Lessons Inspired by Picture Books
for Primary Grades

Purchases of AASL Publications fund advocacy, leadership, professional development, and standards initiatives for school librarians nationally.

ALA Editions purchases fund advocacy, awareness, and accreditation programs for library professionals worldwide.

AASL Standards-Based Learning

Lessons Inspired by Picture Books
for Primary Grades

Maureen Schlosser
and **Rebecca Granatini**

American Association
of School Librarians
TRANSFORMING LEARNING

CHICAGO | 2019

Maureen Schlosser is a retired school librarian who writes for *BookPagez* and blogs for *Knowledge Quest*. She was the cochair of the Nutmeg Book Award and has presented at state and national library conferences. Her articles about integrating the arts with library lessons and advocacy are published in library journals.

Rebecca Granatini is a content-area curriculum specialist with the Wethersfield, Connecticut, Public School System. She has experience teaching grades K–5 and is a Fund for Teachers Fellow. She frequently offers professional development and conference workshops in the areas of STEAM education as well as integrative science and mathematics education.

© 2019 by the American Library Association

Extensive effort has gone into ensuring the reliability of the information in this book; however, the publisher makes no warranty, express or implied, with respect to the material contained herein.

ISBN: 978-0-8389-1775-6 (paper)

Library of Congress Cataloging-in-Publication Data

Names: Schlosser, Maureen, author. | Granatini, Rebecca, author. | American Association of School
    Librarians, associated body.
Title: Lessons inspired by picture books for primary grades / Maureen Schlosser, Rebecca Granatini.
Description: Chicago : ALA Editions, 2019. | Series: AASL standards-based learning | Includes
    bibliographical references and index.
Identifiers: LCCN 2018045329 | ISBN 9780838917756 (print : alk. paper)
Subjects: LCSH: Elementary school libraries—Activity programs. | Picture
    books for children—Educational aspects. | Education—Standards—United States.
Classification: LCC Z675.S3 S2596 2019 | DDC 025.5/4—dc23 LC record available at https://lccn.loc
    .gov/2018045329

Composition by Alejandra Diaz in the Utopia Std and Galano Classic typefaces.

♾ This paper meets the requirements of ANSI/NISO Z39.48–1992 (Permanence of Paper).

Printed in the United States of America
23 22 21 20 19   5 4 3 2 1

For all librarians who truly appreciate
how awesome our profession is.

—M.S.

To the educators who see
the strengths in *all* of their students.
It takes but a spark to develop curiosity in a child.
Thanks for taking the time to inspire learners.

—R.G.

CONTENTS

PREFACE

How a School Librarian and a Classroom Teacher Started Working Together

We are often asked how we developed such a wonderful collaborative relationship. As a classroom teacher, Becky was told to immediately find the media educator—"This person is your connection to the world." Maureen was always seeking new ways to develop media work outside the walls of the school library. It was a match made in heaven. The Crosswalk of the Common Core Standards and the *Standards for the 21st-Century Learner* supported our collaborative work. The documentation guided us as we developed Inquiry lessons to engage all learners. Working together allowed us to support young learners as they synthesized and shared information. The lessons were fun and engaging for everyone.

The response from our first collaborative project was very positive. We continued to dream bigger and bring integrative learning to life throughout our entire school. Twitter, within our building, worked wonders to bring to life what we were doing with our kids. Teachers would stop us in the hallways to inquire about recent tweets and what our kids were up to. When we shared work with families, we invited them in and live-streamed projects so the families could be involved and fully understand our work. The project evolved from there. More and more teachers came on board as they recognized (through our student learning examples) just how valuable this work was. Families shared their children's enthusiasm and began to ask what was next. We were no longer in learning silos where library skills were separate from science and writing skills. All of it became integrated. Best of all, motivation, energy, and excitement went up throughout the school as we all began to look to each other to develop creative and engaging next steps.

When we heard that new *National School Library Standards for Learners, School Librarians, and School Libraries* were on the horizon, we were excited to see how they would support our collaborative work through content areas. The publication did not disappoint us. In fact, we were inspired by how accessible they are to all subjects. We were especially thrilled about the Domains and the Competencies, realizing how they encourage relevant work.

We were excited to start working with the AASL Standards, and like all of our lessons, we began with remarkable picture books. We find that compelling picture books inspire great learning when working with the AASL Standards. We hope this book will save you planning time and demonstrate how to apply the *AASL Standards Framework for Learners* to your future lessons.[1]

WHY THE STANDARDS INSPIRE US

We saw what the lessons did for our kids. Kids who may not have been otherwise engaged were counting down the minutes for our work together. Learners who may not have been seen by peers as "superstars" revealed unique talents and creative ideas. Each student and teacher tapped into their talents, which connected them to something new, something more collaborative, and something that took on a life larger than we could imagine. We learned of our colleagues' talents and experiences that until this moment were hidden. A much-loved kindergarten teacher had been a Macy's Thanksgiving Day Parade balloon handler, and no one had any idea. The kids were thrilled when they heard her firsthand account and her connection to our work with *Balloons Over Broadway.* It was this energy and excitement for learning that prompted us to continue our work together and ultimately to develop this book. We believe that given the opportunity, our entire learning community can be lifted to greatness. School should be an exciting place where we begin the process of developing lifelong learners.

FINDING YOUR COLLABORATIVE PARTNER

Look carefully within your learning community. Who among your colleagues inspires you? Who shares a similar philosophy of teaching and learning? Find an enthusiastic colleague and begin your adventure together. Spend time sharing your philosophy, dream enormous dreams of what your perfect school could be. Then go after it together. If learners are at the heart of your decisions, you can never go wrong. Don't be afraid to dream big.

NOTE

1. American Association of School Librarians, *National School Library Standards for Learners, School Librarians, and School Libraries* (Chicago: ALA Editions, 2018).

ACKNOWLEDGMENTS

e proudly acknowledge the administrators, educators, and parents of the Colchester Public School District in Connecticut. The best lessons in this book were developed with you. Our collaboration fueled projects that made the children so excited to come to school.

Do you remember the day of our first parade? The threat of snow that normally would have brought a school delay or cancellation was ignored. The board of education, administrators, educators, school staff, parents, and children were not going to let impending bad weather cancel the parade. The *Balloons Over Broadway* lesson showed us what happens when learners are encouraged and supported to think, create, share, and grow.

We deeply appreciate the opportunity to write for ALA Editions. It was a true pleasure working with Stephanie Book, manager, communications, for the American Association of School Librarians, and Jamie Santoro, acquisitions editor for ALA Editions. We learned a great deal about writing a manuscript and are thankful for the experience.

We also acknowledge our supportive families who continue to encourage our passion for education.

INTRODUCTION

ithin this book, you will find detailed lessons that support the *AASL Standards Framework for Learners.* Each chapter contains engaging lessons that support the development of learners' competency in a Shared Foundation, including lessons focused on Inquire, Include, Collaborate, Curate, Explore, and Engage. A Shared Foundation is the fundamental component of innovative practices. A Key Commitment at the beginning of each chapter defines the Shared Foundation.

The lessons are divided into four specific Domains to support a Shared Foundation. Each Domain—*Think, Create, Share,* and *Grow*—offers learning experiences with Competencies to assess growth. You'll notice that the "Think" lessons tap into the cognitive Domain and require learners to ask questions, consider background knowledge, read, and evaluate information. Our "Create" lessons mirror the psychomotor Domain as learners activate psychomotor skills by investigating, planning, organizing, and crediting borrowed information. "Share" lessons encompass the affective Domain in which learners practice listening and communicating. The "Grow" lessons echo the developmental Domain, guiding learners to apply learned skills. For an in-depth understanding of the *AASL Standards Framework for Learners,* read AASL's *National School Library Standards for Learners, School Librarians, and School Libraries* and visit the AASL Standards web portal at http://standards .aasl.org.

We invite you to modify our overarching plan. If you want to dip a toe into the *AASL Standards Framework for Learners,* try addressing one Domain. We designed the lessons and assessments to support a single lesson or an entire unit. The rubrics (appendix A) accommodate both scenarios.

GETTING STARTED: OUR TIPS FOR A SMOOTH IMPLEMENTATION

- Begin by exploring the online resources in the materials list. We provide the web addresses at the end of the book in the "Online Resources" section. Consider curating the recommended websites on the home page of the library catalog so learners can easily access these resources.

- Next, make copies of the pre- and post-assessments. You'll realize that they are the same. The results serve as a wonderful artifact to show growth and areas in which to continue work. This will guide you as you address specific learner needs and outcomes.
- Make copies of the worksheets designed for the lessons. The worksheets are at the end of each lesson. Templates that can be modified for your specific needs are located in appendix B. Here you'll find general worksheets like the "Self-Designed Research Activity" to guide personalized exploration on any topic (Appendix B.8).
- Get creative with the anchor charts. Make them appealing to guide discussions and activities. We've provided examples of possible ideas and responses you might hear during a lesson. You may find it useful to keep the anchor charts posted throughout the year to support other lessons.
- Have folders and sticky notes available for lessons. Provide each learner with a folder to hold worksheets and rubrics. Apply sticky notes to pages in the shared text where you'll ask questions. It can be tricky to remember your thread of questioning when interacting with the text. The sticky notes will help you keep your place and stay on track.

INTEGRATING PRACTICES FEATURING THE *AASL STANDARDS FRAMEWORK FOR LEARNERS*

The *AASL Standards Framework for Learners* makes connecting with other standards a breeze. Collaborate with other educators to create crosswalks that work for your learning community. Below are some ideas to make curricular connections of your own.

Our Work with the AASL Standards

Our first collaborative lesson together started with ideas, objectives, and the Crosswalk of the Common Core State Standards and the *Standards for the 21st-Century Learner*. We loved this crosswalk. It proved that working together made sense. We supported each other as we facilitated lessons in which learners asked questions, synthesized information, and shared new learning.

Now our work has changed. We no longer need the crosswalk. Instead, we refer to the *AASL Standards Framework for Learners* and consider curricular connections.[1] We are excited about how the Shared Foundations and Domains can inspire transformative lessons for any content area. Their accessibility to other content-area standards makes for a great point of entry for a collaborative project. In fact, we believe they are among the very best educational standards because at the heart of this work is the learner—a curious, engaged, self-reliant learner.

Tips to Integrate the Framework Today

The following steps are designed to support collaborative lessons and inform your learning community about the *AASL Standards Framework for Learners.*

1. Find a collaborative partner who shares a passion for open-ended learning.
2. Ask what content lessons and standards your partner is currently excited about.
3. Review the *AASL Standards Framework for Learners* (https://standards.aasl.org/learner-framework) and consider what Competencies in the four Domains would work with the lesson. You can start by choosing just one of the Competencies.
4. Share your ideas along with a copy of the *AASL Standards Framework for Learners* to illustrate how the AASL Standards support and enrich classroom learning. Prepare an elevator pitch to explain the framework. Your pitch could be something like this:

   > I loved hearing about your lesson! It had so many connections to the *National School Library Standards.* Take a look! Your lesson ties in perfectly with the Inquire Shared Foundation. A Shared Foundation is the core of innovative lessons. You'll see here that the Shared Foundation is further explained with Key Commitments. Four Domains make up a Shared Foundation. These Domains have Competencies that list observable behaviors for assessment. I can see how this Competency here is perfect for your lesson. What do you think? Is there another Competency that grabs your attention?

5. Collaborate to develop a lesson that involves all learners and works well within time constraints. Invite administrators to the conversation.
6. Assign jobs to gather materials, facilitate lessons, and assess learning.
7. Invite administrators and classroom educators to see the lesson. Distribute flyers that indicate the standards that were met through your work together.
8. Reflect on the entire collaborative experience. Consider what went well and discuss changes for next time. Look at the Competencies and assess learning. Recognize areas that require additional support.
9. Share a celebratory high-five with your collaborative partner on a job well done and start dreaming of your next project!

Cross-Curricular Integration: A Resource Table

We created a Guide to the Standards (table I.1) to indicate how each lesson supports other content-area standards. This guide will help educators and administrators see how valuable the school library is in supporting school achievement.

The table was built by first comparing the *AASL Standards Framework for Learners* with the Next Generation Science Standards (NGSS). We are excited about the NGSS because they offer tremendous opportunities for collaborative work with the classroom educator. Take a moment to check out the website Next Generation Science Standards for States, by States (https://www.nextgenscience.org/), and you'll quickly see how closely the standards connect.

COLLABORATION IS KEY

There is no more perfect way to highlight the importance of AASL's *National School Library Standards* framework and integration of the disciplines than this statement in the College, Career, and Civic Life (C3) Framework for Social Studies State Standards:

> Now more than ever, students need the intellectual power to recognize societal problems; ask good questions and develop robust investigations into them; consider possible solutions and consequences; separate evidence-based claims from parochial opinions; and communicate and act upon what they learn. And most importantly, they must possess the capability and commitment to repeat that process as long as is necessary. Young people need strong tools for, and methods of, clear and disciplined thinking in order to traverse successfully the worlds of college, career, and civic responsibilities.

Source: National Council for the Social Studies (NCSS), *The College, Career, and Civic Life (C3) Framework for Social Studies State Standards: Guidance for Enhancing the Rigor of K–12 Civics, Economics, Geography, and History* (Silver Spring, MD: NCSS, 2013), https://www .socialstudies.org/sites/default/files/c3/C3-Framework-for-Social-Studies.pdf.

Next, we looked closer at how the lessons supported work in social studies, cultural studies, and language arts. Although we have tied specific dimensions within the Inquiry Arc of the *C3 Framework for Social Studies State Standards*, practices from the Next Generation Science Standards (NGSS), and Common Core State Standards (CCSS) for English Language Arts (ELA) to each lesson, a case could be made for many different arrangements to be used in these lessons. We have highlighted those that stood out to us as the most natural connections. Please consider other dimensions, standards, and practices as well. As with everything we offer in our book, this is a guide, intended to be built upon in your collaborative conversations.

★ *Consider how a table such as the Guide to the Standards with alignment to other cross-curricular standards could help you to generate a collaboration with another educator. How exciting it is when all of our work is aligned!*

TABLE I.1

GUIDE TO THE STANDARDS

Lesson/ Book Title	AASL Standards Framework for Learners	Next Generation Science Standards (NGSS)	C3 Framework for Social Studies State Standards	Common Core State Standards for English Language Arts/ Literacy
What Does It Take to Put On a Parade? *Balloons Over Broadway: The True Story of the Puppeteer of Macy's Parade* by Melissa Sweet ▶ Page 1	I.A.1. Learners display curiosity and initiative by formulating questions about a personal interest or a curricular topic. I.B.2. Learners engage with new knowledge by following a process that includes devising and implementing a plan to fill knowledge gaps. I.C.3. Learners adapt, communicate, and exchange learning products with others in a cycle that includes acting on feedback to improve. I.D.3. Learners participate in an ongoing inquiry-based process by enacting new understanding through real-world connections.	**Practice 1** **Asking Questions and Defining Problems** Ask questions based on observations to find more information about the natural and/or designed world (K–2). Ask questions about what would happen if a variable is changed (3–5). Ask and/or identify questions that can be answered by an investigation (K–2). Ask scientific (testable) and non-scientific (non-testable) questions (3–5). **Practice 6** **Construct an Explanation and Design Solutions** Use tools and/or materials to design or build a device that solves a specific problem or a solution to a specific problem. Apply scientific idea to solve a design problem.	**Inquiry Arc Dimension One** **Development of Questions and the Planning of Inquiries** The way to tie all of this content together is through the use of compelling and supporting questions. **Inquiry Arc Dimension Two** **Applying Disciplinary Concepts and Tools** Working with a robust compelling question and a set of discrete supporting questions, teachers and students determine the kind of content they need in order to develop their inquiries. Students access disciplinary knowledge both to develop questions and to pursue those questions using disciplinary concepts and tools.	Reading Standards 1–10 Writing Standard 7 Speaking and Listening Standard 1 Language Standard 6 **Shared Language:** Explanation; Point of View; Analysis; Argument; Evidence; Questioning

Lesson/ Book Title	AASL Standards Framework for Learners	Next Generation Science Standards (NGSS)	C3 Framework for Social Studies State Standards	Common Core State Standards for English Language Arts/ Literacy
How Can We Reduce Waste? *Compost Stew: An A to Z Recipe for the Earth* by Mary McKenna Siddals ⊙ Page 13	I.A.1. Learners display curiosity and initiative by formulating questions about a personal interest or a curricular topic. I.B.1. Learners engage with new knowledge by following a process that includes using evidence to investigate questions. I.C.4. Learners adapt, communicate, and exchange learning products with others in a cycle that includes sharing products with an authentic audience. I.D.4. Learners participate in an ongoing inquiry-based process by using reflection to guide informed decisions.	**Practice 1** **Asking Questions and Defining Problems** Ask questions that can be investigated and predict reasonable outcomes based on patterns such as cause and effect relationships.	**Inquiry Arc Dimension One** **Development of Questions and the Planning of Inquiries** The way to tie all of this content together is through the use of compelling and supporting questions. **Inquiry Arc Dimension Two** **Applying Disciplinary Concepts and Tools** Working with a robust compelling question and a set of discrete supporting questions, teachers and students determine the kind of content they need in order to develop their inquiries. Students access disciplinary knowledge both to develop questions and to pursue those questions using disciplinary concepts and tools.	Reading Standards 1–10 Writing Standard 7 Speaking and Listening Standard 1 Language Standard 6 **Shared Language:** Explanation; Point of View; Analysis; Argument; Evidence; Questioning

Lesson/ Book Title	AASL Standards Framework for Learners	Next Generation Science Standards (NGSS)	C3 Framework for Social Studies State Standards	Common Core State Standards for English Language Arts/ Literacy
How Can We Record Our Observations? *Me . . . Jane* by Patrick McDonnell > Page 23	I.A.1. Learners display curiosity and initiative by formulating questions about a personal interest or a curricular topic. I.B.2. Learners engage with new knowledge by following a process that includes devising and implementing a plan to fill knowledge gaps. I.C.4. Learners adapt, communicate, and exchange learning products with others in a cycle that includes sharing products with an authentic audience. I.D.3. Learners participate in an ongoing inquiry-based process by enacting new understanding through real-world connections.	**Practice 1** **Asking Questions and Defining Problems** Ask questions based on observations to find more information about the natural and/or designed world (K–2). Ask and/or identify questions that can be answered by an investigation (K–2). Ask scientific (testable) and non-scientific (non-testable) questions (3–5).	**Inquiry Arc Dimension One** **Development of Questions and the Planning of Inquiries** The way to tie all of this content together is through the use of compelling and supporting questions. **Inquiry Arc Dimension Four** **Communicating Conclusions and Taking Informed Action** Demonstrate understanding through a variety of means, including a range of venues and a variety of forms (e.g., discussions, debates, policy analyses, video productions, and portfolios). Moreover, the manner in which students work to create their solutions can differ.	Reading Standard 1 Writing Standards 1–8 Speaking and Listening Standards 1–6 **Shared Language:** Argument; Explanation; Sources; Evidence; Claims; Counterclaims; Visually/Visualize; Credibility; Questioning; Point of View

Lesson/ Book Title	AASL Standards Framework for Learners	Next Generation Science Standards (NGSS)	C3 Framework for Social Studies State Standards	Common Core State Standards for English Language Arts/ Literacy
What Influences People to Live and Work in Our Community? *Town Is by the Sea* by Joanne Schwartz ▶ Page 34	I.A.2. Learners display curiosity and initiative by recalling prior and background knowledge as context for new meaning. I.B.3. Learners engage with new knowledge by following a process that includes generating products that illustrate learning. I.C.2. Learners adapt, communicate, and exchange learning products with others in a cycle that includes providing constructive feedback. I.D.3. Learners participate in an ongoing inquiry-based process by enacting new understanding through real-world connections.	**Practice 1** **Asking Questions and Defining Problems** Ask questions based on observations to find more information about the natural and/or designed world (K–2). Ask and/or identify questions that can be answered by an investigation (K–2). Ask scientific (testable) and non-scientific (non-testable) questions (3–5).	**Inquiry Arc Dimension One** **Development of Questions and the Planning of Inquiries** The way to tie all of this content together is through the use of compelling and supporting questions. **Inquiry Arc Dimension Two** **Applying Disciplinary Concepts and Tools** Working with a robust compelling question and a set of discrete supporting questions, teachers and students determine the kind of content they need in order to develop their inquiries. Students access disciplinary knowledge both to develop questions and to pursue those questions using disciplinary concepts and tools.	Reading Standards 1–10 Writing Standard 7 Speaking and Listening Standard 1 Language Standard 6 **Shared Language:** Explanation; Point of View; Analysis; Argument; Evidence; Questioning

Lesson/ Book Title	AASL Standards Framework for Learners	Next Generation Science Standards (NGSS)	C3 Framework for Social Studies State Standards	Common Core State Standards for English Language Arts/ Literacy
What Can We Learn about a Society by Understanding How Students Get to School? *The Way to School* by Rosemary McCarney ⊙ Page 45	II.A.3. Learners contribute a balanced perspective when participating in a learning community by describing their understanding of cultural relevancy and placement within the global learning community. II.B.3. Learners adjust their awareness of the global learning community by representing diverse perspectives during learning activities. II.C.2. Learners exhibit empathy with and tolerance for diverse ideas by contributing to discussions in which multiple viewpoints on a topic are expressed. II.D.3. Learners demonstrate empathy and equity in knowledge building within the global learning community by reflecting on their own place within the global learning community.	**Practice 1** **Asking Questions and Defining Problems** Ask questions based on observations to find more information about the natural and/or designed world (K–2). Ask and/or identify questions that can be answered by an investigation (K–2). Ask scientific (testable) and non-scientific (non-testable) questions (3–5). *Note: Scientific focus could be on the role of the geography of a region and available resources.*	**Inquiry Arc Dimension Two** **Applying Disciplinary Concepts and Tools** Working with a robust compelling question and a set of discrete supporting questions, teachers and students determine the kind of content they need in order to develop their inquiries. Students access disciplinary knowledge both to develop questions and to pursue those questions using disciplinary concepts and tools. **Inquiry Arc Dimension Four** **Communicating Conclusions and Taking Informed Action** Demonstrate understanding through a range of venues, including a variety of forms (e.g., discussions, debates, policy analyses, video productions, and portfolios). Moreover, the manner in which students work to create their solutions can differ.	Reading Standards 1–10 Writing Standards 1–8 Speaking and Listening Standards 1–6 Language Standard 6 **Shared Language:** Analysis; Argument; Evidence; Questioning; Explanation; Sources; Claims; Counterclaims; Visually/Visualize; Credibility

Lesson/ Book Title	AASL Standards Framework for Learners	Next Generation Science Standards (NGSS)	C3 Framework for Social Studies State Standards	Common Core State Standards for English Language Arts/ Literacy
How Do People Determine What They Want and What They Need? *I Like, I Don't Like* by Anna Baccelliere ⊙ Page 60	II.A.2. Learners contribute a balanced perspective when participating in a learning community by adopting a discerning stance toward points of view and opinions expressed in information resources and learning products. II.B.1. Learners adjust their awareness of the global learning community by interacting with learners who reflect a range of perspectives. II.C.1. Learners exhibit empathy with and tolerance for diverse ideas by engaging in informed conversation and active debate. II.D.3. Learners demonstrate empathy and equity in knowledge building within the global learning community by reflecting on their own place within the global learning community.	**Practice 7** **Engaging in Argument from Evidence** Compare and refine arguments based on an evaluation of the evidence presented. Distinguish among facts, reasoned judgment based on research findings, and speculation in an explanation. Construct and/or support an argument with evidence, data, and/or a model.	**Inquiry Arc Dimension Two** **Applying Disciplinary Concepts and Tools** Working with a robust compelling question and a set of discrete supporting questions, teachers and students determine the kind of content they need in order to develop their inquiries. Students access disciplinary knowledge both to develop questions and to pursue those questions using disciplinary concepts and tools. **Inquiry Arc Dimension Three** **Evaluating Sources and Using Evidence** Helping students develop a capacity for gathering and evaluating sources and then using evidence in disciplinary ways.	Reading Standards 1–10 Writing Standards 1, 2, 7–10 Speaking and Listening Standard 1 Language Standard 6 **Shared Language:** Analysis; Argument; Evidence; Questioning; Sources; Claims; Counterclaims; Gather

Lesson/ Book Title	AASL Standards Framework for Learners	Next Generation Science Standards (NGSS)	C3 Framework for Social Studies State Standards	Common Core State Standards for English Language Arts/ Literacy
How Do People Decide Where to Live? *Why Am I Here?* by Constance Ørbeck-Nilssen ▶ Page 70	II.A.3. Learners contribute a balanced perspective when participating in a learning community by describing their understanding of cultural relevancy and placement within the global learning community. II.B.1. Learners adjust their awareness of the global learning community by interacting with learners who reflect a range of perspectives. II.C.1. Learners exhibit empathy with and tolerance for diverse ideas by engaging in informed conversation and active debate. II.D.2. Learners demonstrate empathy and equity in knowledge building within the global learning community by demonstrating interest in other perspectives during learning activities.	**Practice 1** **Asking Questions and Defining Problems** Ask questions based on observations to find more information about the natural and/or designed world (K–2). Ask and/or identify questions that can be answered by an investigation (K–2). Ask scientific (testable) and non-scientific (non-testable) questions (3–5). *Note: Scientific focus could be on the role of the geography of a region and available resources.*	**Inquiry Arc Dimension Four** **Communicating Conclusions and Taking Informed Action** Demonstrate understanding through a variety of means, including a range of venues and a variety of forms (e.g., discussions, debates, policy analyses, video productions, and portfolios). Moreover, the manner in which students work to create their solutions can differ.	Reading Standard 1 Writing Standards 1–8 Speaking and Listening Standards 1–6 **Shared Language:** Argument; Explanation; Sources; Evidence; Claims; Counterclaims; Visually/Visualize; Credibility

Lesson/ Book Title	AASL Standards Framework for Learners	Next Generation Science Standards (NGSS)	C3 Framework for Social Studies State Standards	Common Core State Standards for English Language Arts/ Literacy
What Do Statues Represent? *Her Right Foot* by David Eggers ▶ Page 84	II.A.2. Learners contribute a balanced perspective when participating in a learning community by adopting a discerning stance toward points of view and opinions expressed in information resources and learning products. II.B.1. Learners adjust their awareness of the global learning community by interacting with learners who reflect a range of perspectives. II.C.2. Learners exhibit empathy with and tolerance for diverse ideas by contributing to discussions in which multiple viewpoints on a topic are expressed. II.D.2. Learners demonstrate empathy and equity in knowledge building within the global learning community by demonstrating interest in other perspectives during learning activities.	**Practice 8** **Obtaining, Evaluating, and Communicating Information** Communicate information or design ideas and/ or solutions with others in oral and/ or written forms using models, drawings, writing, or numbers that provide detail about scientific ideas, practices, and/or design ideas.	**Inquiry Arc Dimension Two** **Applying Disciplinary Concepts and Tools** Working with a robust compelling question and a set of discrete supporting questions, teachers and students determine the kind of content they need in order to develop their inquiries. Students access disciplinary knowledge both to develop questions and to pursue those questions using disciplinary concepts and tools.	Reading Standards 1–10 Writing Standard 7 Speaking and Listening Standard 1S Language Standard 6 **Shared Language:** Questioning; Explanation; Point of View; Analysis; Argument; Evidence

Lesson/ Book Title	AASL Standards Framework for Learners	Next Generation Science Standards (NGSS)	C3 Framework for Social Studies State Standards	Common Core State Standards for English Language Arts/ Literacy
What Makes a Team Successful? *How to Build a Plane: A Soaring Adventure of Mechanics, Teamwork, and Friendship* **by Saskia Lacey** ▶ Page 99	III.A.3. Learners identify collaborative opportunities by deciding to solve problems informed by group interaction. III.B.2. Learners participate in personal, social, and intellectual networks by establishing connections with other learners to build on their own prior knowledge and create new knowledge III.C.1. Learners work productively with others to solve problems by soliciting and responding to feedback from others. III.D.2. Learners actively participate with others in learning situations by recognizing learning as a social responsibility.	**Practice 1** **Asking Questions and Defining Problems** Ask questions about what would happen if a variable is changed. Identify scientific (testable) and non-scientific (non-testable) questions. Ask questions based on observations to find more information about the natural and/or designed world.	**Inquiry Arc Dimension One** **Development of Questions and the Planning of Inquiries** The way to tie all of this content together is through the use of compelling and supporting questions. **Inquiry Arc Dimension Two** **Applying Disciplinary Concepts and Tools** Working with a robust compelling question and a set of discrete supporting questions, teachers and students determine the kind of content they need in order to develop their inquiries. Students access disciplinary knowledge both to develop questions and to pursue those questions using disciplinary concepts and tools.	Reading Standards 1–10 Writing Standard 7 Speaking and Listening Standard 1S Language Standard 6 **Shared Language:** Explanation; Point of View; Analysis; Argument; Evidence; Questioning

Lesson/ Book Title	AASL Standards Framework for Learners	Next Generation Science Standards (NGSS)	C3 Framework for Social Studies State Standards	Common Core State Standards for English Language Arts/ Literacy
How Can Listening to Ideas Help Us Develop a Successful Plan? *Shh! We Have a Plan* by Chris Haughton ⊙ Page 113	III.A.3. Learners identify collaborative opportunities by deciding to solve problems informed by group interaction. III.B.2. Learners participate in personal, social, and intellectual networks by establishing connections with other learners to build on their own prior knowledge and create new knowledge. III.C.1. Learners work productively with others to solve problems by soliciting and responding to feedback from others. III.D.1. Learners actively participate with others in learning situations by actively contributing to group discussions.	**Practice 3** **Planning and Carrying Out Investigations** Evaluate appropriate methods and/or tools for collecting data. Make a prediction about what would happen if a variable changed. **Practice 8** **Obtaining, Evaluating, and Communicating Information** Communicate information or design ideas and/or solutions with others in oral and/or written forms using models, drawings, writing, or numbers that provide detail about scientific ideas, practices, and/or design ideas.	**Inquiry Arc Dimension Four** **Communicating Conclusions and Taking Informed Action** Demonstrate understanding through a variety of means, including a range of venues and a variety of forms (e.g., discussions, debates, policy analyses, video productions, and portfolios). Moreover, the manner in which students work to create their solutions can differ.	Reading Standard 1 Writing Standards 1–8 Speaking and Listening Standards 1–6 **Shared Language:** Argument; Explanation; Sources; Evidence; Claims; Counterclaims; Visually/Visualize; Credibility

Lesson/ Book Title	AASL Standards Framework for Learners	Next Generation Science Standards (NGSS)	C3 Framework for Social Studies State Standards	Common Core State Standards for English Language Arts/ Literacy
How Can We Work Together to Repurpose Materials? *The Branch* by Mireille Messier ▶ Page 127	III.A.2. Learners identify collaborative opportunities by developing new understandings through engagement in a learning group. III.B.2. Learners participate in personal, social, and intellectual networks by establishing connections with other learners to build on their own prior knowledge and create new knowledge. III.C.1. Learners work productively with others to solve problems by soliciting and responding to feedback from others. III.D.1. Learners actively participate with others in learning situations by actively contributing to group discussions.	**Practice 6** **Constructing Explanations and Designing Solutions** Apply scientific ideas to solve design problems. Generate and/or compare multiple solutions to a problem. **Practice 8** **Obtaining, Evaluating, and Communicating Information** Communicate information or design ideas and/ or solutions with others in oral and/ or written forms using models, drawings, writing, or numbers that provide detail about scientific ideas, practices, and/or design ideas.	**Inquiry Arc Dimension Four** **Communicating Conclusions and Taking Informed Action** Demonstrate understanding through a variety of means, including a range of venues and a variety of forms (e.g., discussions, debates, policy analyses, video productions, and portfolios). Moreover, the manner in which students work to create their solutions can differ.	Reading Standard 1 Writing Standards 1–8 Speaking and Listening Standards 1–6 **Shared Language:** Argument; Explanation; Sources; Evidence; Claims; Counterclaims; Visually/Visualize

Lesson/ Book Title	AASL Standards Framework for Learners	Next Generation Science Standards (NGSS)	C3 Framework for Social Studies State Standards	Common Core State Standards for English Language Arts/ Literacy
How Can We Collect Important Information to Share with Others? *Antsy Ansel: Ansel Adams, a Life in Nature* by Cindy Jenson-Elliott ▶ Page 135	IV.A.1. Learners act on an information need by determining the need to gather information. IV.B.1 Learners gather information appropriate to the task by seeking a variety of sources. IV.C.2. Learners exchange information resources within and beyond their learning community by contributing to collaboratively constructed information sites by ethically using and reproducing others' work. IV.D.1. Learners select and organize information for a variety of audiences by performing ongoing analysis of and reflection on the quality, usefulness, and accuracy of curated resources.	**Practice 4** **Analyzing and Interpreting Data** Observe thoughts and ideas and record information. Compare and contrast data collected by different groups in order to discuss similar and different findings.	**Inquiry Arc Dimension Two** **Applying Disciplinary Concepts and Tools** Working with a robust compelling question and a set of discrete supporting questions, teachers and students determine the kind of content they need in order to develop their inquiries. Students access disciplinary knowledge both to develop questions and to pursue those questions using disciplinary concepts and tools. **Inquiry Arc Dimension Four** **Communicating Conclusions and Taking Informed Action** Demonstrate understanding through a variety of means, including a range of venues and a variety of forms (e.g., discussions, debates, policy analyses, video productions, and portfolios). Moreover, the manner in which students work to create their solutions can differ.	Reading Standards 1–10 Writing Standards 1–8 Speaking and Listening Standards 1–6 Language Standard 6 **Shared Language:** Analysis; Argument; Evidence; Questioning; Explanation; Sources; Claims; Counterclaims; Visually/Visualize; Credibility

Lesson/ Book Title	AASL Standards Framework for Learners	Next Generation Science Standards (NGSS)	C3 Framework for Social Studies State Standards	Common Core State Standards for English Language Arts/ Literacy
Why Is It Important to Keep Track of What We Read and What We Want to Read? *Wanted! Ralfy Rabbit, Book Burglar* by Emily MacKenzie ⊙ Page 148	IV.A.1. Learners act on an information need by determining the need to gather information. IV.B.4. Learners gather information appropriate to the task by organizing information by priority, topic, or other systematic scheme. IV.C.3. Learners exchange information resources within and beyond their learning community by joining with others to compare and contrast information derived from collaboratively constructed information sites. IV.D.3. Learners select and organize information for a variety of audiences by openly communicating curation processes for others to use, interpret, and validate.	**Practice 1** **Asking Questions and Defining Problems** Ask questions based on observations to find more information about the natural and/or designed world (K–2).	**Inquiry Arc Dimension Two** **Applying Disciplinary Concepts and Tools** Working with a robust compelling question and a set of discrete supporting questions, teachers and students determine the kind of content they need in order to develop their inquiries. Students access disciplinary knowledge both to develop questions and to pursue those questions using disciplinary concepts and tools.	Reading Standards 1–10 Writing Standard 7 Speaking and Listening Standard 1 Language Standard 6 **Shared Language:** Analysis; Argument; Evidence; Questioning

Lesson/ Book Title	AASL Standards Framework for Learners	Next Generation Science Standards (NGSS)	C3 Framework for Social Studies State Standards	Common Core State Standards for English Language Arts/ Literacy
Why Is It Important to Use Multiple Sources to Learn about a Topic? *Thirsty, Thirsty Elephants* by Sandra Markle ⊙ Page 158	IV.A.1. Learners act on an information need by determining the need to gather information. IV.B.3. Learners gather information appropriate to the task by systematically questioning and assessing the validity and accuracy of information. IV.C.3. Learners exchange information resources within and beyond their learning community by joining with others to compare and contrast information derived from collaboratively constructed information sites. IV.D.3. Learners select and organize information for a variety of audiences by openly communicating curation processes for others to use, interpret, and validate.	**Practice 7** **Engaging in Argument from Evidence** Distinguish between opinions and evidence in one's own explanations. Distinguish between explanations that account for all gathered evidence and those that do not. Distinguish among facts, reasoned judgment based on research findings, and speculations.	**Inquiry Arc Dimension Three** **Evaluating Sources and Using Evidence** Helping students develop a capacity for gathering and evaluating sources and then using evidence in disciplinary ways.	Reading Standards 1–10 Writing Standards 1, 2, 7–10 Developing Claims and Speaking and Listening Standard 1 **Shared Language:** Argument; Sources; Evidence; Claims; Counterclaims; Gather

Lesson/ Book Title	AASL Standards Framework for Learners	Next Generation Science Standards (NGSS)	C3 Framework for Social Studies State Standards	Common Core State Standards for English Language Arts/ Literacy
How Do People and Groups Decide How to Make the World a Better Place? *Ada's Violin: The Story of the Recycled Orchestra of Paraguay* by Susan Hood Page 171	V.A.1. Learners develop and satisfy personal curiosity by reading widely and deeply in multiple formats and write and create for a variety of purposes. V.B.1. Learners construct new knowledge by problem solving through cycles of design, implementation, and reflection. V.C.3. Learners engage with the learning community by collaboratively identifying innovative solutions to a challenge or problem. V.D.2. Learners develop through experience and reflection by recognizing capabilities and skills that can be developed, improved, and expanded.	**Practice 1** **Asking Questions and Defining Problems** Ask questions based on observations to find more information about the natural and/or designed world (K–2). Ask questions about what would happen if a variable is changed (3–5). Ask and/or identify questions that can be answered by an investigation (K–2). **Practice 6** **Constructing Explanations and Designing Solutions** Use tools and/ or materials to design or build a device that solves a specific problem or a solution to a specific problem. Apply scientific ideas to solve a design problem.	**Inquiry Arc Dimension Two** **Applying Disciplinary Concepts and Tools** Working with a robust compelling question and a set of discrete supporting questions, teachers and students determine the kind of content they need in order to develop their inquiries. Students access disciplinary knowledge both to develop questions and to pursue those questions using disciplinary concepts and tools. **Inquiry Arc Dimension Four** **Communicating Conclusions and Taking Informed Action** Demonstrate understanding through a variety of means, including a range of venues and a variety of forms (e.g., discussions, debates, policy analyses, video productions, and portfolios). Moreover, the manner in which students work to create their solutions can differ.	Reading Standards 1–10 Writing Standards 1–8 Speaking and Listening Standards 1–6 Language Standard 6 **Shared Language:** Analysis; Argument; Evidence; Questioning; Explanation; Sources; Claims; Counterclaims; Visually/Visualize

Lesson/ Book Title	AASL Standards Framework for Learners	Next Generation Science Standards (NGSS)	C3 Framework for Social Studies State Standards	Common Core State Standards for English Language Arts/ Literacy
How Can People Identify Problems? *Follow the Moon Home: A Tale of One Idea, Twenty Kids, and a Hundred Sea Turtles* by Philippe Cousteau ⊙ Page 183	V.A.3. Learners develop and satisfy personal curiosity by engaging in inquiry-based processes for personal growth. V.B.1. Learners construct new knowledge by problem solving through cycles of design, implementation, and reflection. V.C.2. Learners engage with the learning community by co-constructing innovative means of investigation. V.D.2. Learners develop through experience and reflection by recognizing capabilities and skills that can be developed, improved, and expanded.	**Practice 6** **Constructing Explanations and Designing Solutions** Make observations (firsthand or from media) to construct an evidence-based account for natural phenomena. Generate and/or compare multiple solutions to a problem. Construct an explanation of observed relationships. Identify the evidence that supports particular points in an explanation.	**Inquiry Arc Dimension Four** **Communicating Conclusions and Taking Informed Action** Demonstrate understanding through a variety of means, including a range of venues and a variety of forms (e.g., discussions, debates, policy analyses, video productions, and portfolios). Moreover, the manner in which students work to create their solutions can differ.	Reading Standard 1 Writing Standards 1–8 Speaking and Listening Standards 1–6 **Shared Language:** Argument; Explanation; Sources; Evidence; Claims; Counterclaims; Visually/Visualize

Lesson/ Book Title	AASL Standards Framework for Learners	Next Generation Science Standards (NGSS)	C3 Framework for Social Studies State Standards	Common Core State Standards for English Language Arts/ Literacy
How Can People Find Solutions to Problems in Their Community? *One Plastic Bag: Isatou Ceesay and the Recycling Women of the Gambia* by Miranda Paul ⊙ Page 195	V.A.3. Learners develop and satisfy personal curiosity by engaging in inquiry-based processes for personal growth. V.B.2. Learners construct new knowledge by persisting through self-directed pursuits by tinkering and making. V.C.1. Learners engage with the learning community by expressing curiosity about a topic of personal interest or curricular relevance. V.D.3. Learners develop through experience and reflection by open-mindedly accepting feedback for positive and constructive growth.	**Practice 1** **Asking Questions and Defining Problems** Use prior knowledge to describe problems that can be solved. Define a simple design problem that can be solved through the development of a process or system and includes several criteria for success. **Practice 6** **Constructing Explanations and Designing Solutions** Apply scientific ideas to solve design problems. Generate and/or compare multiple solutions to a problem. Construct an explanation of observed relationships.	**Inquiry Arc Dimension Four** **Communicating Conclusions and Taking Informed Action** Demonstrate understanding through a variety of means, including a range of venues and a variety of forms (e.g., discussions, debates, policy analyses, video productions, and portfolios). Moreover, the manner in which students work to create their solutions can differ.	Reading Standard 1 Writing Standards 1–8 Speaking and Listening Standards 1–6 **Shared Language:** Argument; Explanation; Sources; Evidence; Claims; Counterclaims; Visually/Visualize; Credibility

Lesson/ Book Title	AASL Standards Framework for Learners	Next Generation Science Standards (NGSS)	C3 Framework for Social Studies State Standards	Common Core State Standards for English Language Arts/ Literacy
Why Is It Important to Find Innovative Solutions to Problems? *Farmer Will Allen and the Growing Table* by Jacqueline Briggs Martin Page 205	V.A.3. Learners develop and satisfy personal curiosity by engaging in inquiry-based processes for personal growth. V.B.2. Learners construct new knowledge by persisting through self-directed pursuits by tinkering and making. V.C.3. Learners engage with the learning community by collaboratively identifying innovative solutions to a challenge or problem. V.D.3. Learners develop through experience and reflection by open-mindedly accepting feedback for positive and constructive growth.	**Practice 6** **Constructing Explanations and Designing Solutions** Use tools and/ or materials to design a solution to a specific problem Apply scientific ideas to solve a design problem.	**Inquiry Arc Dimension Four** **Communicating Conclusions and Taking Informed Action** Demonstrate understanding through a variety of means, including a range of venues and a variety of forms (e.g., discussions, debates, policy analyses, video productions, and portfolios). Moreover, the manner in which students work to create their solutions can differ.	Reading Standard 1 Writing Standards 1–8 Speaking and Listening Standards 1–6 **Shared Language:** Argument; Explanation; Sources; Evidence; Claims; Counterclaims; Visually/Visualize; Credibility

Lesson/ Book Title	AASL Standards Framework for Learners	Next Generation Science Standards (NGSS)	C3 Framework for Social Studies State Standards	Common Core State Standards for English Language Arts/ Literacy
How Does Our Background Influence Perception? *They All Saw a Cat* by Brendan Wenzel ⊙ Page 215	VI.A.3. Learners follow ethical and legal guidelines for gathering and using information by evaluating information for accuracy, validity, social and cultural context, and appropriateness for need. VI.B.2. Learners use valid information and reasoned conclusions to make ethical decisions in the creation of knowledge by acknowledging authorship and demonstrating respect for the intellectual property of others. VI.C.2. Learners responsibly, ethically, and legally share new information with a global community by disseminating new knowledge through means appropriate for the intended audience. VI.D.1. Learners engage with information to extend personal learning by personalizing their use of information and information technologies.	**Practice 1** **Asking Questions and Defining Problems** Ask questions based on observations to find more information about the natural and/or designed world (K–2). Ask and/or identify questions that can be answered by an investigation (K–2).	**Inquiry Arc Dimension Three** **Evaluating Sources and Using Evidence** Helping students develop a capacity for gathering and evaluating sources and then using evidence in disciplinary ways.	Reading Standards 1–10 Writing Standards 1, 2, 7–10 Developing Claims and Speaking and Listening Standard 1 **Shared Language:** Argument; Sources; Evidence; Claims; Counterclaims; Gather

Lesson/ Book Title	AASL Standards Framework for Learners	Next Generation Science Standards (NGSS)	C3 Framework for Social Studies State Standards	Common Core State Standards for English Language Arts/ Literacy
What Causes People to Have Certain Feelings about Different Animals? *Fox's Garden* by Princesse Camcam ⊙ Page 225	VI.A.3. Learners follow ethical and legal guidelines for gathering and using information by evaluating information for accuracy, validity, social and cultural context, and appropriateness for need. VI.B.2. Learners use valid information and reasoned conclusions to make ethical decisions in the creation of knowledge by acknowledging authorship and demonstrating respect for the intellectual property of others. VI.C.2. Learners responsibly, ethically, and legally share new information with a global community by disseminating new knowledge through means appropriate for the intended audience. VI.D.3. Learners engage with information to extend personal learning by inspiring others to engage in safe, responsible, ethical, and legal information behaviors.	**Practice 1** **Asking Questions and Defining Problems** Ask questions based on observations to find more information about the natural and/or designed world (K–2). Ask and/or identify questions that can be answered by an investigation (K–2).	**Inquiry Arc Dimension Two** **Applying Disciplinary Concepts and Tools** Working with a robust compelling question and a set of discrete supporting questions, teachers and students determine the kind of content they need in order to develop their inquiries. Students access disciplinary knowledge both to develop questions and to pursue those questions using disciplinary concepts and tools. **Inquiry Arc Dimension Three** **Evaluating Sources and Using Evidence** Helping students develop a capacity for gathering and evaluating sources and then using evidence in disciplinary ways.	Reading Standards 1–10 Writing Standards 1, 2, 7–10 Speaking and Listening Standard 1 Language Standard 6 **Shared Language:** Analysis; Argument; Evidence; Questioning; Claims; Counterclaims; Gather

Lesson/ Book Title	AASL Standards Framework for Learners	Next Generation Science Standards (NGSS)	C3 Framework for Social Studies State Standards	Common Core State Standards for English Language Arts/ Literacy
Who Owns an Idea? *In the Bag! Margaret Knight Wraps It Up* by Monica Kulling ▶ Page 235	VI.A.2. Learners follow ethical and legal guidelines for gathering and using information by understanding the ethical use of information, technology, and media. VI.B.2. Learners use valid information and reasoned conclusions to make ethical decisions in the creation of knowledge by acknowledging authorship and demonstrating respect for the intellectual property of others. VI.C.1. Learners responsibly, ethically, and legally share new information with a global community by sharing information resources in accordance with modification, reuse, and remix policies. VI.D.2. Learners engage with information to extend personal learning by reflecting on the process of ethical generation of knowledge.	**Practice 1** **Asking Questions and Defining Problems** Ask questions based on observations to find more information about the natural and/or designed world (K–2). Ask and/or identify questions that can be answered by an investigation (K–2).	**Inquiry Arc Dimension Three** **Evaluating Sources and Using Evidence** Helping students develop a capacity for gathering and evaluating sources and then using evidence in disciplinary ways. **Inquiry Arc Dimension Four** **Communicating Conclusions and Taking Informed Action** Demonstrate understanding through a variety of means, including a range of venues and a variety of forms (e.g., discussions, debates, policy analyses, video productions, and portfolios). Moreover, the manner in which students work to create their solutions can differ.	Reading Standards 1–10 Writing Standards 1, 2, 7–10 Developing Claims and Speaking and Listening Standard 1 **Shared Language:** Argument; Sources; Evidence; Claims; Counterclaims; Gather

ADDITIONAL RESOURCES

C3 Framework for Social Studies State Standards: https://www.socialstudies.org/sites/default/files/c3/C3-Framework-for-Social-Studies.pdf

CCSS English Language Arts–College and Career Readiness Anchor Standards for Reading: www.corestandards.org/ELA-Literacy/CCRA/R/

Next Generation Science Standards (NGSS): www.nextgenscience.org/search-standards (search by "practices" as indicated in this document)

NOTE

1. American Association of School Librarians, *AASL Standards Framework for Learners* (Chicago: ALA Editions, 2018).

CHAPTER 1

Inquire Lessons

KEY COMMITMENT
Build new knowledge by inquiring, thinking critically, identifying
problems, and developing strategies for solving problems.

WHAT DOES IT TAKE TO PUT ON A PARADE?

Shared Foundation: Inquire
Featured Book: *Balloons Over Broadway:
The True Story of the Puppeteer of Macy's
Parade* by Melissa Sweet

Summary

If someone asked you to build something for
a parade, what would you make? What obsta-
cles would you need to consider? Puppeteer Tony Sarg tackled these questions as
he thought about the Macy's parade. He wondered how he could make puppets
large enough for everyone to enjoy. Sarg worked through a design process to create
colossal helium balloon puppets. We see them floating in the sky every year in the
Macy's parade. Author Melissa Sweet delivers the fascinating story of Sarg's design
process. Readers will see how Sarg worked through the Think, Create, Share, and
Grow Domains in the *National School Library Standards.* Learners will apply new
knowledge to put on a parade of their own.

Pre-Assessment

- Pass out the "What Does It Take to Put On a Parade?" worksheet (WS 1.1).
- Ask learners to highlight or circle "Pre-Assessment" at the top of the worksheet.
- Direct learners to write a list of things to consider when planning a parade.

- Save worksheets to establish a baseline for Competencies.
- Establish a baseline for learning using the "Inquire Create Competencies Rubric" (Appendix A.1).

> 📌 *Designate one color marker to grade pre-assessments and a different color to assess post-assessments. The rubrics are the same, so this method will help you differentiate between the results.*

THINK LESSON

Objective
Learners will ask questions about planning a parade.

AASL Standards Framework for Learners: I.A.1. Learners display curiosity and initiative by formulating questions about a personal interest or a curricular topic.

Lesson Duration
45–50 minutes

Materials
- "Our Questions about Putting On a Parade" anchor chart (AC 1.1)
- Markers
- Pencils
- Copy of *Balloons Over Broadway: The True Story of the Puppeteer of Macy's Parade* by Melissa Sweet
- "Questions I Have about Planning a Parade" worksheet (WS 1.2)
- "Inquire Think Competencies Rubric" (Appendix A.1)

> 📌 *Invite classroom educators and administrators to hear about a fun lesson plan that parents and board members will love. Share assessments and standard connections. They'll jump right in to work with you.*

Our Questions about Putting On a Parade

» How are floats chosen for a parade?

» Where do the people in the parade come from? How are they selected?

» How are floats built?

» Who builds the floats?

» How do people decide to have a parade?

» How are parades advertised? How do people know where parades will happen?

» When do people start practicing for their parade?

» What do they do to practice?

» Why do people have parades?

Lesson

1. Tell learners that you have exciting news. They will be putting on their own parade! Explain that there is a lot to think about when planning a parade. You will read a book to help them consider what they might need for their event.

2. Introduce *Balloons Over Broadway: The True Story of the Puppeteer of Macy's Parade.* Read the title and look at the illustration. Ask learners what they expect to learn from this book.

3. Explain that while you read, their job is to ask questions about planning parades.

4. As you read, ask learners the following questions and write responses on the "Our Questions about Putting On a Parade" anchor chart (AC 1.1):
   - "What questions do you have for Macy's about parade preparations?" (p. 6)
   - "What questions do you have about the parade route?" (p. 7)
   - "What questions did Tony Sarg ask? Why did he ask them?" (pp. 10–11)
   - "What question is Tony Sarg asking on this page? Why is the question important?" (p. 15)
   - "What questions does Tony Sarg ask on this page? Why should we pay attention to his questions when planning a parade?" (p. 20)
   - "If you had a chance to interview Tony Sarg about the parade, what would you ask him?" (p. 28)

5. Finish the story and tell learners that it's time to start planning their parade.

6. Pass out the "Questions I Have about Planning a Parade" worksheet to each learner (WS 1.2).

7. Read the directions with learners.

8. Collect finished work to assess Competencies using the "Inquire Think Competencies Rubric" (Appendix A.1).

★ *Who will watch the parade? It could be a small venue with one grade level or a large event with the entire school!*

CREATE LESSON

Objective

Learners will choose a theme for the parade, join a parade committee, and start planning next steps.

AASL Standards Framework for Learners: I.B.2. Learners engage with new knowledge by following a process that includes devising and implementing a plan to fill knowledge gaps.

Lesson Duration

2 lessons, 45–50 minutes each

Materials

- "Parade Themes" anchor chart (AC 1.2)
- "Parade Committees" anchor chart (AC 1.3)
- Sticky notes
- Pencils
- Access to online videos and images about the Macy's parade
- "Parade Idea" worksheet (WS 1.3)
- "Planning Sheet" worksheet (Appendix B.1)
- "Inquire Create Competencies Rubric" (Appendix A.1)

Volunteers

You will need volunteers for the following lessons. Ask parents, grandparents, other educators, administrators, and board members to get involved in this fun project. Volunteers will provide support as learners create and implement a plan for the parade.

Lesson Day 1

1. Gather learners in front of the "Parade Themes" anchor chart (AC 1.2).
2. Discuss some of the questions learners had about planning a parade.
3. Say, "Some of you asked about the theme of the parade. A theme is an idea that everything in the parade will connect to. Let's think about a theme that has

> ## 🌑 Parade Themes
>
> » Veterans/Heroes
> » Animals
> » Inventions/Innovations
> » Things We Are Thankful For
> » Things We Have Learned About
>
> » Our Community
> » Book Characters
> » Our Favorite Things
> » Fall
> » The Great Outdoors

meaning for our school. We can think about upcoming events and holidays, the school motto, our favorite things, or possibly a STEAM theme."

4. Write ideas on the "Parade Themes" anchor chart (AC 1.2).
5. Have learners vote for a favorite theme with a show of hands.
6. Ask learners to think about what should be in the parade that works with the theme. Encourage them to think about other parades and brainstorm ideas.
7. Pass out the "Parade Idea" worksheet (WS 1.3). Read directions.
8. Give learners a chance to walk around and see all illustrations.

Lesson Day 2

1. Tell learners that after looking at their illustrations, you noticed drawings of floats, marching bands, dancers, cheerleaders, and lots of costumes.
2. Explain that learners will join a Parade Committee to plan the parade. They have four choices based on their illustrations (for example, Float Committee, Marching Band Committee, Dance Committee, and Advertising Committee).
3. Have learners write their names on sticky notes, and place the notes on the "Parade Committees" anchor chart (AC 1.3) under a committee of their choice. If one committee has too many learners, ask for volunteers to switch to another group.
4. Show videos of parades that highlight marching bands, dancers, and floats. Show pictures of flyers, posters, and newspaper articles announcing the parade. Find newspaper articles on the Library of Congress website.
5. Ask learners what they notice about the videos and pictures. What ideas can they incorporate?
6. Pass out the "Planning Sheet" worksheet (Appendix B.1).
7. Send learners to meet with their Committee Chairperson—an educator, an administrator, or a parent volunteer.
8. Committee Chairs will ask guiding questions to help learners create a plan.
9. Collect finished work to assess Competencies using the "Inquire Create Competencies Rubric" (Appendix A.1).

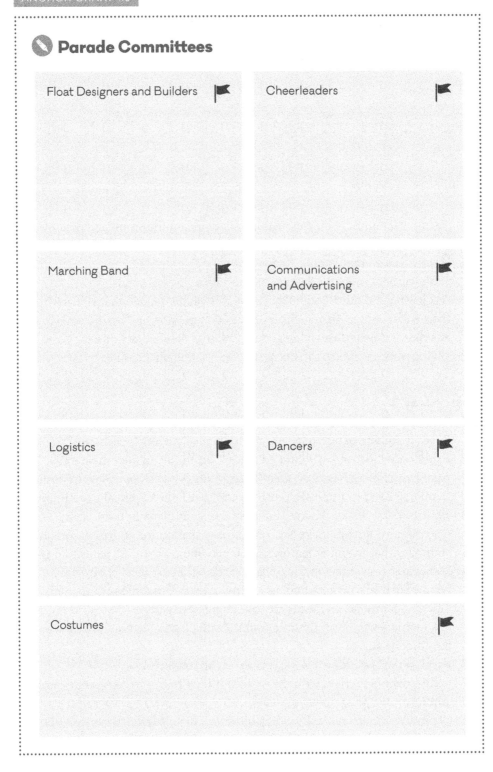

Parade Committees

Float Designers and Builders 🚩	Cheerleaders 🚩
Marching Band 🚩	Communications and Advertising 🚩
Logistics 🚩	Dancers 🚩
Costumes 🚩	

SHARE LESSON

Objective
Learners will make posters, send invitations, build floats, practice dances and music, and march in a parade.

AASL Standards Framework for Learners: I.C.3. Learners adapt, communicate, and exchange learning products with others in a cycle that includes acting on feedback to improve.

Lesson Duration
3–4 hours and time for the parade

Materials
- Boxes
- Duct tape
- Scissors
- Paint
- Decorative materials and fabric
- Wagons and carts
- Construction paper
- Staplers

- Video recording equipment
- Sticky notes
- Pencils
- "Parade Feedback" anchor chart (AC 1.4)
- "Inquire Share Competencies Rubric" (Appendix A.1)

> ★ *Start making floats with a sturdy foundation or platform that will fit on a wagon. Remind learners that the float must fit through doors and hallways.*

Lesson
1. Tell learners that now is the time to bring their plans to life. They will make their posters, write announcements, build floats, make costumes, and practice marching and dancing. All of this will happen with the help of volunteers and any available educators. Prompt volunteers to ask learners guiding questions about their projects rather than telling them what to do.
2. Practice marching in the parade route. Mark stopping points along the way for performances.
3. Invite the school, parents, and board members to watch the parade with flyers, posters, and e-mail notices made by learners.

4. Reflect with learners about the parade when it is over. Ask learners to consider what went well when preparing for and presenting the parade. What problems did they run into? What changes would they make? Ask learners to write their ideas on sticky notes and add them to the "Parade Feedback" anchor chart (AC 1.4). Direct learners to add their names to the sticky notes.

5. Review the sticky notes to assess Competencies using the "Inquire Share Competencies Rubric" (Appendix A.1).

ANCHOR CHART 1.4

Parade Feedback

What went well?

Problems:

Suggestions for next year:

GROW LESSON

Objective
Learners will reflect on their parade work.

AASL Standards Framework for Learners: I.D.3. Learners participate in an ongoing inquiry-based process by enacting new understanding through real-world connections.

Lesson Duration
45 minutes

Materials
- "Reflect and Grow" worksheet (Appendix B.2)
- Pencils
- "Inquire Grow Competencies Rubric" (Appendix A.1)

Lesson
1. Ask learners to consider the planning process for the parade. What parts did they enjoy? What parts did they struggle with? What did they learn about themselves as a committee member?
2. Pass out the "Reflect and Grow" worksheets and ask learners to respond to the questions (Appendix B.2).
3. Collect finished work to assess Competencies using the "Inquire Grow Competencies Rubric" (Appendix A.1).

Post-Assessment
- Remind learners that before they started their parade work, they were asked what it takes to put on a parade. Explain that we are going to see what they learned now that they have planned a parade of their own.
- Pass out the "What Does It Take to Put On a Parade?" worksheet (WS 1.1). Read the directions together.
- Direct learners to circle the word "Post-Assessment" at the top of the page to distinguish this from the initial assessment.
- Assess learning with the "Inquire Create Competencies Rubric" (Appendix A.1). Compare results with the pre-assessment.

WHAT DOES IT TAKE TO PUT ON A PARADE?

Name: _____

Pre-Assessment/Post-Assessment

Directions: Your town needs help planning a parade. What should the planners think about to make sure the parade is a success? List your ideas below.

1) _____

_____

_____

2) _____

_____

_____

3) _____

_____

_____

4) _____

_____

_____

5) _____

_____

_____

QUESTIONS I HAVE ABOUT PLANNING A PARADE

Name: _____

Directions: What questions do you have about planning a parade? Write your questions below.

1) _____

_____

2) _____

_____

3) _____

_____

4) _____

_____

5) _____

_____

6) _____

_____

PARADE IDEA

Name: _____

Directions: Draw a picture of what you would like to see in the parade. Think about the parade theme before illustrating. Write about your drawing on the lines below.

_____

_____

_____

_____

HOW CAN WE REDUCE WASTE?

Shared Foundation: Inquire
Featured Book: *Compost Stew: An A to Z Recipe for the Earth* by Mary McKenna Siddals

Summary

Many of us love to eat a good stew, especially on a cold, wintery night. But no matter how cold and hungry you are, you'll definitely want to take a pass on a plate of compost stew. Mary McKenna Siddals, the author of *Compost Stew: An A to Z Recipe for the Earth,* creatively informs readers about the ingredients in this brew. Using a sing-song narrative, Siddals works through the alphabet to share a healthy earth recipe that everyone can follow. The illustrations, created with collage, prove to be an appropriate medium for a book about scraps. Learners will look at leftovers differently after reading *Compost Stew.* They'll also think about the food they throw away and consider composting as a way to reduce trash and help our world. This is the perfect book to motivate learners to make a difference.

Pre-Assessment

- Explain to learners that you would like to find out what they know about reducing garbage.
- Pass out "Reducing Garbage" worksheet for learners to complete (WS 1.4). Ask learners to highlight or circle "Pre-Assessment" at the top of the worksheet.
- Look for gaps in knowledge about composting and asking questions.
- Assess skills with the "Inquire Think Competencies Rubric" (Appendix A.1).

THINK LESSON

Objective
Learners will generate questions about garbage while looking at pictures of cafeteria waste and dump sites.

AASL Standards Framework for Learners: I.A.1. Learners display curiosity and initiative by formulating questions about a personal interest or a curricular topic.

Lesson Duration
45 minutes

Materials

- Pictures of garbage from the school cafeteria
- Pictures of dump sites
- Projector
- Computer or mobile device
- "What Do I Notice about Garbage?" anchor chart (AC 1.5)

- Markers
- "What Do I Wonder about Garbage?" worksheet (WS 1.5)
- Pencils
- "Inquire Think Competencies Rubric" (Appendix A.1)

ANCHOR CHART 1.5

 What Do I Notice about Garbage?

1. A lot of food is thrown away.
2. There are lots of plastic bags and containers.
3. Some packages are not opened.
4. Whole apples and bananas are thrown away.
5. Sandwiches with one bite are in the garbage.

 *Looking for a safe place for learners to find images? Try **Photos for Class**. Learners are reminded to give credit to images on this site.*

Lesson

1. Show a picture of the cafeteria garbage. Tell learners the photograph was taken in their cafeteria.
2. Give learners time to think about what they notice. Invite them to share their observations with a neighbor. Write responses on the "What Do I Notice about Garbage?" anchor chart (AC 1.5).
3. Show pictures of garbage dumps.
4. Ask learners to carefully look at the images. What do they notice? Write responses on the "What Do I Notice about Garbage?" anchor chart (AC 1.5).
5. Tell learners it's time to write questions about the garbage they studied.
6. Pass out the "What Do I Wonder about Garbage?" worksheet (WS 1.5).
7. Assess work with the "Inquire Think Competencies Rubric" (Appendix A.1).

CREATE LESSON

Objective

Learners will find answers to their questions about garbage.

AASL Standards Framework for Learners: I.B.1. Learners engage with new knowledge by following a process that includes using evidence to investigate questions.

Lesson Duration
2 lessons, 45 minutes each

Materials
- "KWL Chart" anchor chart (AC 1.6)
- Markers
- Copy of *Compost Stew: An A to Z Recipe for the Earth* by Mary McKenna Siddals
- Access to library website with links to databases and online resources
- Books about composting
- Sticky notes
- Pencils
- "Inquire Create Competencies Rubric" (Appendix A.1)

ANCHOR CHART 1.6

KWL Chart

I Know . . .	I Wonder . . .	I Learned . . .
» I know that compost is made from food scraps.	» I wonder if all food can be composted? » Does compost smell? » Does it attract bugs? » How long does it take food to decompose? » Do you have to take care of compost?	» I learned that some foods cannot be composted. » I learned that paper can go in a compost bin. » Worms help decompose food. » Tea bags can go in a compost pile. » Compost is good for the Earth.

Lesson Day 1

1. Explain that many learners noticed that a lot of garbage gets thrown away every day in the cafeteria.

2. Ask, "I wonder what we can do to make a difference? Let's read *Compost Stew: An A to Z Recipe for the Earth* by Mary McKenna Siddals and see if we can get some ideas."

3. As you read the story, ask the following questions:
   - "What can we expect to learn from this book? What do you know about compost?" (cover) Write responses in the "I Know" column of the "KWL Chart" anchor chart.
   - "What questions do you have?" (p. 1) Write the questions in the "I Wonder" column on the "KWL Chart" anchor chart.
   - "What's happening so far? Why is the author mentioning food we find in the garbage?" (p. 5)
   - "What questions do you have after reading this page?" (p. 7) Write the questions in the "I Wonder" column on the "KWL Chart" anchor chart.
   - "What is happening on these pages? What questions do you have?" (pp. 24–25) Write responses in the "I Wonder" column on the "KWL Chart" anchor chart.
   - "What did you learn from the author's note? What questions do you have?" (author's note) Give learners a chance to turn and talk with their neighbor. Add responses to the chart.

Lesson Day 2

1. Tell learners that today they are going to find answers to their questions on the "KWL Chart" anchor chart about compost.

2. Use library databases that learners are familiar with. Gather books for learners to read.

3. Use sticky notes to add new learning to the "KWL Chart" anchor chart (AC 1.6). Tell learners to write their initials on their posts. Collect this information to assess learning using the "Inquire Create Competencies Rubric" (Appendix A.1).

SHARE LESSON

Objective
Learners will collect discarded fruits and vegetables in the cafeteria for composting.

AASL Standards Framework for Learners: I.C.4. Learners adapt, communicate, and exchange learning products with others in a cycle that includes sharing products with an authentic audience.

Lesson Duration
30–40 Minutes

Materials
- Garbage bin on wheels
- Compost bin
- Leaves and branches
- Shovel
- Classroom volunteers
- Poster paper
- Markers
- Pencils
- "What Goes in a Compost Bin?" anchor chart (AC 1.7)
- "Inquire Share Competencies Rubric" (Appendix A.1)

★ *Can't get your hands on a garbage bin with wheels? No problem! A bucket will do! What about a compost bin? Ask the PTO to fund the project or apply for grant money. Still no funds? Make a compost bin out of large storage bins!*

ANCHOR CHART 1.7

🚫 **What Goes in a Compost Bin?**

» Apples
» Bananas
» Eggshells
» Vegetables
» Nut shells

Lesson

1. Talk to administrators, custodians, and cafeteria staff before the lesson. Ask permission to set up a compost bin outside. Decide as a team where to put the compost bin.
2. Meet with learners in the cafeteria.
3. Ask, "How can composting make a difference with the garbage in the cafeteria?"
4. Explain to learners that they will start composting.
5. Show learners the compost bin.
6. Explain that you will put leaves and branches on the bottom of the bin once you move it outside. Why is that? *Adding leaves, branches, and water to the fruit and vegetable scraps breaks down the food.*
7. Ask, "What can we put in the compost bin?" Write responses on the "What Goes in a Compost Bin?" anchor chart (AC 1.7).
8. Explain that when lunchtime is over, volunteers will collect food scraps.
9. Dump the scraps in the compost bin. Mix the compost with a shovel.
10. Ask learners to make posters that explain what food can go in the compost bin. Collect posters before hanging them in the cafeteria to assess learning using the "Inquire Share Competencies Rubric" (Appendix A.1).

GROW LESSON

Objective
Learners will observe the amount of scraps collected for the compost bin.

AASL Standards Framework for Learners: I.D.4. Learners participate in an ongoing inquiry-based process by using reflection to guide informed decisions.

Lesson Duration
40 minutes

Materials
- "Observations and Reflections" worksheet (WS 1.6)
- Pencils
- Photo of garbage from first lesson
- Photo of garbage after composting unit
- Projector
- Computer or mobile device
- "How Did We Do?" anchor chart (AC 1.8)
- Markers
- "Inquire Grow Competencies Rubric" (Appendix A.1)

> **How Did We Do?**

» There is less food in the garbage.

» The amount of garbage is reduced.

» No fruits or vegetables were thrown away.

★ *Have fun sorting through trash with **Garbology**, an interactive sorting game that learners will love.*

Lesson

1. Show learners the photo of garbage from the first lesson. Explain this is what the garbage looked like before they did their composting work.
2. Show learners a more recent image of the garbage. What do they notice? How did this experience change the way they think about their lunch? Record responses on the "How Did We Do?" anchor chart (AC 1.8).
3. Pass out the "Observations and Reflections" worksheet (WS 1.6). Ask learners to answer the questions.
4. Assess learning with "Inquire Grow Competencies Rubric" (Appendix A.1).

Post-Assessment

- Inform learners that you would like to find out how much they learned about reducing garbage.
- Pass out the "Reducing Garbage" worksheet (WS 1.4).
- Direct learners to circle the word "Post-Assessment" at the top of the page to distinguish this from the initial assessment.
- Use the "Inquire Think Competencies Rubric" and compare results with the pre-assessment (Appendix A.1).

WORKSHEET 1.4

REDUCING GARBAGE

Name: _____

Pre-Assessment/Post-Assessment

Directions: What do you know about reducing garbage? What do you wonder about garbage? Record your answers and questions in the garbage bin below.

I know . . . _____

_____

_____

_____

_____

I wonder . . . _____

_____

_____

_____

_____

WHAT DO I WONDER ABOUT GARBAGE?

Name: _____

What do I wonder about garbage in the cafeteria?

What do I wonder about landfill stations?

OBSERVATIONS AND REFLECTIONS

1) What do I notice?

_____

_____

_____

_____

_____

2) What difference does it make?

_____

_____

_____

_____

_____

3) What will I do now?

_____

_____

_____

_____

_____

HOW CAN WE RECORD OUR OBSERVATIONS?

Shared Foundation: Inquire
Featured Book: *Me . . . Jane* by Patrick McDonnell

Summary

Take a moment to step outside. What do you see? What do you hear? What do you wonder? Nature offers tremendous opportunities to wonder about the world around us. Jane Goodall understood this idea as a young child. *Me . . . Jane* tells the story of Goodall's youth. She was fascinated by nature and drew pictures, wrote labels, took notes, and asked questions about what she observed. Learners will see the value in Goodall's note-taking habits when her accomplishments are revealed at the end of the story. A new interest in appreciating the world outside the classroom will grow after reading this book.

Pre-Assessment

- Form groups of learners.
- Give each group an item from nature (feathers, shells, rocks, pinecones, etc.).
- Pass out a blank sheet of paper. Ask learners to write their names at the top of the page.
- Ask learners to write "Pre-Assessment" at the top of the worksheet.
- Explain that they are to study the object from nature and record their observations and questions.
- Assess learning with the "Inquire Think Competencies Rubric" (Appendix A.1). Save results to measure growth at the end of the unit with the post-assessment.

THINK LESSON

Objective

After noticing how inquisitive Jane Goodall is about nature, learners will generate questions about animals.

AASL Standards Framework for Learners: I.A.1. Learners display curiosity and initiative by formulating questions about a personal interest or a curricular topic.

Lesson Duration

45 minutes

Materials

- Paper
- Pencils
- Clipboards
- Access to an online animal website or database
- Projector
- Computer or mobile device

- "What Do Scientists Do?" anchor chart (AC 1.9)
- Markers
- "What I Notice, What I Wonder" worksheet (Appendix B.3)
- "Inquire Think Competencies Rubric" (Appendix A.1)

ANCHOR CHART 1.9

What Do Scientists Do?

» Watch	» Take notes	» Ask questions
» Learn	» Make lists	» Wonder
» Study	» Draw pictures	» Observe
» Read	» Write labels	» Experience the world

Lesson

1. Ask learners, "Think of a time when you were curious about something. What were you wondering about?" Explain that you will read a story about a girl who was very curious about animals. Add that her name is Jane Goodall, and today she is a famous scientist who made great discoveries about chimpanzees.

2. Say, "Let's learn about Jane and observe how she acts like a scientist."

3. As you read, ask learners the following questions and record responses on the "What Do Scientists Do?" anchor chart (AC 1.9):
   - What can you infer about Jane while looking at this childhood photograph? (front endpaper)
   - What is Jane doing on these pages? (pp. 4–5)
   - How is Jane acting like a scientist? (pp. 5–6)
   - What do you notice about Jane's notes? (pp. 7–8)
   - What is Jane doing on this page? (p. 13)
   - How is Jane acting like a scientist? (pp. 14–19)
   - What was Jane's dream?

4. Tell learners that it is their turn to act like scientists. They will visit a library database or favorite animal website and view the images and video clips. Instruct learners to record their questions on the "What I Notice, What I Wonder" worksheet (Appendix B.3).

5. Pass out clipboards, pencils, and the "What I Notice, What I Wonder" worksheet (Appendix B.3).
6. Collect worksheets and assess learning with the "Inquire Think Competencies Rubric" (Appendix A.1).

CREATE LESSON

Objective
Learners will create a plan to find answers to their questions.

AASL Standards Framework for Learners: I.B.2. Learners engage with new knowledge by following a process that includes devising and implementing a plan to fill knowledge gaps.

Lesson Duration
2 lessons, 40–50 minutes each

Materials
- "How Can We Find Answers?" anchor chart (AC 1.10)
- Markers
- "Animal Research Plan" worksheet (WS 1.7)
- Pencils
- Computer lab or mobile devices
- Access to library databases and recommended animal websites
- Projector
- Access to library books
- Completed "What I Notice, What I Wonder" worksheet from previous lesson (Appendix B.3)
- "Inquire Create Competencies Rubric" (Appendix A.1)

Ask volunteers to help learners find books on shelves and navigate the Internet. Senior citizens, grandparents, parents, and high school students offer young researchers essential support.

 How Can We Find Answers?

Library Catalog
- » Search for our library website (write web address here).
- » Click on the library catalog.
- » Type the name of the animal in the search bar.
- » Find a book you want to check out and make sure it is available.
- » Write the title of the book and the call number.

Databases and Websites
- » Search for our library website (write web address here).
- » Read descriptions of websites and databases.
- » Click on links about animals.

Passwords
- » (Write the names of databases and their passwords here.)

Lesson Day 1

1. Say, "The last time we were together, we observed and wondered about animals. Let's take a moment to share some of our questions and observations." Ask learners to turn and talk with their neighbor and express their thoughts.
2. Ask, "How can we find answers to your questions?"
3. Explain that today, you will show them how to access library resources. After seeing what's available, learners will create a plan to find answers to their questions about animals.
4. Write the web address of the library website on the "How Can We Find Answers?" anchor chart (AC 1.10). Model how to access the library website. Point to the library catalog and explain its purpose. Model how to open the library catalog, type in a search term, and read book descriptions. Point to the call number and the title of a book. Tell learners to write the title and call number of a book they want to read. Explain that with this information, you can help them find the book on the shelf.
5. Demonstrate how to find their answers on databases and websites. Click on the library website. Point to the databases and websites. Write passwords for any databases on the "How Can We Find Answers?" anchor chart (AC 1.10).
6. Say, "Now that I have highlighted some resources, it's time to start planning your research. How will you find answers to your questions? What resources will you use?"

7. Pass out the "Animal Research Plan" worksheet (WS 1.7).
8. Collect worksheets at the end of the lesson. Use the "Inquire Create Competencies Rubric" to assess learning (Appendix A.1). Staple each student's "Animal Research Plan" worksheet (WS 1.7) and "What I Notice, What I Wonder" worksheet (Appendix B.3) together. Save worksheets for the next lesson.

Lesson Day 2

1. Engage learners by asking them to describe how to get to the library website. Follow their directions.
2. Explain that today they will find answers to their questions by following the plan they drafted in the previous lesson.
3. Pass out their stapled worksheets—"What I Notice, What I Wonder" (Appendix B.3) and "Animal Research Plan" (WS 1.7).
4. Ask volunteers to assist learners who need help navigating websites and finding books.
5. Tell learners they can write the answers to their questions on the back of their worksheets.

SHARE LESSON

Objective
Learners will share information about their animal in a creative way.

AASL Standards Framework for Learners: I.C.4. Learners adapt, communicate, and exchange learning products with others in a cycle that includes sharing products with an authentic audience.

Lesson Duration
2–3 class sessions, 40–50 minutes each

Now for the fun part. Ask the music teacher, the art teacher, and the physical education teacher to help with this part of the lesson.

★ *Curate links to poetry guides and music on your library website.*
Poets.org, *an AASL Best Website for Teaching and Learning, has a helpful*
"Poetic Forms" page. **MusicQuest**, *an AASL Best App for Teaching and*
Learning, allows learners to create their own tunes both online and with
the app.

Materials

- "Animal Research Plan" (WS 1.7) and "What I Notice, What I Wonder" (Appendix B.3) worksheets
- "How Can We Share Our Learning?" anchor chart (AC 1.11)
- Sticky notes
- Pencils
- Volunteers
- "Inquire Share Competencies Rubric" (Appendix A.1)
- Library stations set up ahead of time:
  - Music station
  - Laptops or mobile devices
  - Headphones
  - Links to music platforms, like *MusicQuest,* curated on library website, and apps like *GarageBand,* an **AASL Best App for Teaching and Learning**
  - Paper
  - Pencils
  - Tablets with a favorite content creation app (try the *Tellagami* app, an **AASL Best App for Teaching and Learning**)
  - Arts and crafts station
    - ▫ Miscellaneous craft materials (glue, watercolor paints, crayons, etc.)
  - Poetry station
    - ▫ Poetry templates: "Haiku Poem" (Appendix B.4), "Theme Poem" (Appendix B.5), and "Acrostic Poem" (Appendix B.6)
    - ▫ Science-themed poetry books
    - ▫ Paper
    - ▫ Pencils
    - ▫ Crayons
    - ▫ Markers
- "Animal Research Plan" worksheet from previous lesson (WS 1.7)
- "What I Notice, What I Wonder" worksheet from previous lesson (Appendix B.3)

ANCHOR CHART 1.11

How Can We Share Our Learning?

Poetry

Technology

Music

Movement

Art

★ *Hold a quick meeting with volunteers before this lesson to describe the activities. Show the volunteers how to access online materials and use apps.*

Lesson

1. Invite learners to share fun facts about their animals.
2. Ask, "How can we inform others about what we learned?" Brainstorm ideas and write them on the "How Can We Share Our Learning?" anchor chart (AC 1.11).
3. Describe the different stations.
4. Tell learners to write their names on a sticky note and choose how they want to share their information. Limit each station to a workable number of learners to accommodate space and supplies.
5. Return the "Animal Research Plan" (WS 1.7) and the "What I Notice, What I Wonder" (Appendix B.3) worksheets so learners can review their information.
6. Send the groups to the library stations where an educator or volunteer will introduce the materials and give instructions to access and use the online resources and apps.
7. Review products to assess learning using the "Inquire Share Competencies Rubric" (Appendix A.1).

GROW LESSON

Objective

Learners will make observations about organizations that inspire students to contribute to society.

AASL Standards Framework for Learners: I.D.3. Learners participate in an ongoing inquiry-based process by enacting new understanding through real-world connections.

Lesson Duration

45–55 minutes

Materials

- "Making a Difference" anchor chart (AC 1.12)
- Access to the following websites (see "Online Resources" for web addresses at the end of the book):

– Jane Goodall's Roots and Shoots
– *Youth Service America*
– "Citizen Scientists: Resources to Find the Perfect Project," a *Knowledge Quest* blog post

- Computer lab or mobile devices
- Projector
- "What I Notice, What I Wonder" worksheet (Appendix B.3)
- Pencils
- "Inquire Grow Competencies Rubric" (Appendix A.1)

📌 *Curate links for this lesson on your library website with the heading "Make a Difference."*

Lesson

1. Ask, "Did your animal research inspire you to take action? What ideas do you have? Today, we are going to look at a few websites that highlight students who are making a difference."
2. Write the following websites on the "Making a Difference" anchor chart (AC 1.12) and model how to open them from the library website. The web addresses are listed in the "Online Resources" section at the end of the book.
   – Jane Goodall's Roots and Shoots
   – Youth Service America
   – "Citizen Scientists: Resources to Find the Perfect Project," a *Knowledge Quest* blog post
3. As you explore the websites together, ask learners what they notice. Write ideas on the "Making a Difference" anchor chart (AC 1.12).
4. Tell learners to choose one website to explore. They will write the title of the website in the "Topic" section of the "What I Notice, What I Wonder" worksheet (Appendix B.3). Direct learners to record observations and questions.
5. Explain that learners should not register for any campaigns or projects. If they see a project they like, they can make note of it on their "What I Notice, What I Wonder" worksheet (Appendix B.3).
6. Save worksheets to assess learning with the "Inquire Grow Competencies Rubric" (Appendix A.1).

Post-Assessment

- Distribute nature items that learners observed at the beginning of the unit (feathers, shells, rocks, pinecones, etc.).
- Pass out a blank sheet of paper to each student. Direct learners to write their names at the top of the page. Ask them to write the word "Post-Assessment" at the top of the page to distinguish this from the initial assessment.
- Explain that they will record their observations and questions on the sheet of paper.
- Assess learning with the "Inquire Think Competencies Rubric" (Appendix A.1) and compare results with the pre-assessment.

ANCHOR CHART 1.12

🌀 Making a Difference

Jane Goodall's Roots and Shoots
https://www.rootsandshoots.org/aboutus

_____

_____

Youth Service America
https://ysa.org/

_____

_____

Knowledge Quest—"Citizen Scientists: Resources to Find the Perfect Project"
http://knowledgequest.aasl.org/citizen-scientists-resources-find-perfect-project/

_____

_____

ANIMAL RESEARCH PLAN

Name: _____

Pre-Assessment/Post-Assessment

What will I need?

- _____   - _____
- _____   - _____
- _____   - _____

Where will I find information about my animal?

_____

_____

_____

How will I access the information?

_____

_____

_____

What steps do I need to take?

- _____   - _____
- _____   - _____
- _____   - _____

WHAT INFLUENCES PEOPLE TO LIVE AND WORK IN OUR COMMUNITY?

Shared Foundation: Inquire
Featured Book: *Town Is by the Sea*
by Joanne Schwartz

Summary

Imagine a drone with a video camera flying over your town for one day. What would the recording reveal? What does an average day look like for your town? In *Town Is by the Sea* by Joanne Schwartz, we learn about a day in the life of a mining town. The father spends his day working below the ground while his son plays above ground along the seashore. The profound illustrations highlight the contrast of the different settings, exposing why the family lives by the sea. After reading this story, learners will wonder about the location of their town and think about what would make people want to move and work where they live.

Pre-Assessment

- Pass out the "Our Town" worksheet (WS 1.8).
- Ask learners to highlight or circle "Pre-Assessment" at the top of the worksheet.
- Direct learners to respond to the questions.
- Assess learners' desire to learn about the town using the "Inquire Grow Competencies Rubric" (Appendix A.1).

THINK LESSON

Objective

After reading *Town Is by the Sea* by Joanne Schwartz, learners will look at an aerial view of their town, describe the location, and wonder why people live and work there.

AASL Standards Framework for Learners: I.A.2. Learners display curiosity and initiative by recalling prior and background knowledge as context for new meaning.

Lesson Duration

2 lessons, 45–50 minutes each

Materials

- Copy of *Town Is by the Sea* by Joanne Schwartz
- Access to the Internet
- Projector with computer or mobile device
- Access to an interactive online mapping tool
- Pencils
- "Collecting Information about Our Town" anchor chart (AC 1.13)
- "Venn Diagram" worksheet (Appendix B.7)
- "Inquire Think Competencies Rubric" (Appendix A.1)

ANCHOR CHART 1.13

Collecting Information about Our Town

What Do You Already Know about Our Town?

» We have schools.

» There is a town library.

» We have grocery stores.

» We have shopping malls.

» There is a Main Street with shopping and restaurants.

» Our town is small.

» Our town has a lot of buildings.

What Do You Notice About Our Town?

» Our homes are by the . . .

» Our businesses are by the . . .

» Our town is by the . . .

Lesson Day 1

1. Introduce the story by reading the title and asking learners to look at the illustration. Ask, "What can we expect this book to be about?"

2. Tell learners that as you read the story, you would like them to compare the town in the story with their town. Ask, "What do you already know about your town?" Write the answers on the "Collecting Information about Our Town" anchor chart (AC 1.13).

3. Say, "Let's read this story and see how different this town is from where we live."

4. As you read the story, ask the following questions:
   - "What do you notice about this page?" (title page)
   - "What can you see from your house?" (p. 1)

- "Notice how the author describes the town using four words. How would you describe our town using this same pattern?" (p. 2)
- "What questions do you have about this page?" (p. 5)
- "What do your mornings sound like?" (p. 6)
- "What do you see along the road near your house?" (p. 7)
- "What do you notice about the illustration? How does it compare to the illustration on the previous page?" (pp. 10–11)
- "What do you see when you are on a swing?" (pp. 16–17)
- "What do you notice about these pages?" (pp. 18–19)
- "How far away is Main Street from his home? How can you tell?" (p. 22)
- "There is a pattern in this book. Have you noticed it yet? What is it?" (p. 26)
- "What did you learn about the grandfather?" (pp. 28–29)
- "How do you think the father feels about his job? How can you tell?" (pp. 36–43)
- "What did you learn about the boy's future on these pages?" (pp. 45–47)

5. Say, "Compare the town by the sea with our town. What is the same? What is different? You are going to create a Venn Diagram to compare and contrast the two places."
6. Pass out the "Venn Diagram" worksheet (Appendix B.7). Tell learners to label one part of the Venn Diagram with *Town Is by the Sea* and label the other part with the name of their town.
7. Save work to assess learning with the "Inquire Think Competencies Rubric" (Appendix A.1).

Lesson Day 2

1. Introduce the lesson by saying, "Give me a thumbs-up sign if you have ever looked at a map of our town. Today we are going to use an online mapping tool to see what we notice about our town."
2. Demonstrate how to use an online mapping tool. In the search bar, type the name of your town and state.
3. Explore the map together using tools to highlight points. Ask the following questions and write learners' responses on the "Collecting Information about Our Town" anchor chart (AC 1.13).
   - "What do you notice about our town?"
   - "Where is it located? What is it near?"
   - "What do you notice about the businesses? Where are they located? What are they near?"
   - "What do you notice about the schools? The neighborhoods?"
   - "Why do you think people live and work here?"

4. Give learners a chance to explore their town using an online mapping tool.

CREATE LESSON

Objective
Learners will create a marketing campaign to persuade people to live and work in their community.

AASL Standards Framework for Learners: I.B.3. Learners engage with new knowledge by following a process that includes generating products that illustrate learning.

Lesson Duration
3 lessons, 45–50 minutes each

> 📌 *Open Google Maps and type the name of your town. You'll see your town highlighted in red. Trace, copy, or print the map for projects.*

Materials
- "Marketing Ideas" anchor chart (AC 1.14)
- "Planning Sheet" (Appendix B.1)
- "Inquire Create Competencies Rubric" (Appendix A.1)
- Curated examples of promotional cartoon maps, brochures, posters, and commercials for towns on library website (try using *Piktochart,* an **AASL Best Website for Teaching and Learning,** to present the resources with a beautiful design)
- Library stations set up ahead of time:
  - "Creating Cartoon Maps" center
    - Butcher paper
    - Laptops or mobile devices
    - Access to examples of cartoon maps
    - Markers
    - Crayons
    - Pencils
    - Town maps
  - "Creating Brochures and Posters" center
    - Laptops
    - Access to examples of brochures of towns
    - Printer
    - Paper
    - Crayons
    - Markers

– "Creating Commercials" center
- ◻ Green screen or green butcher paper taped to wall
- ◻ Mobile devices with green screen app
- ◻ Video recording equipment
- ◻ Access to examples of tourism commercials

- Volunteers

★ *No volunteers? Meet with tech-savvy learners ahead of time and demonstrate how to use the equipment. They can assist other learners as they create their products.*

 Marketing Ideas

Who: Who is our audience?
- » Families
- » Senior citizens
- » College graduates

What: What products will we make?
- » Commercials
- » Brochures
- » Cartoon maps
- » Posters

When: When will we share our marketing materials?
- » Spring

Where: Where will we share our products?
- » Chamber of commerce
- » Restaurants
- » Shops on Main Street

How: How will we share our marketing products?
- » Invite the chamber of commerce and town officials to see the marketing products
- » Distribute materials to local stores
- » Ask the public television station to consider showing commercials

Lesson Day 1

1. Introduce the lesson by telling learners that the mayor wants more people to move to their town and work. Ask, "How can we persuade people to move here?" Write ideas on the "Marketing Ideas" anchor chart (AC 1.14).
2. Explain that it is always a good idea to create an advertising plan before getting to work. Ask the following questions and write answers on the "Marketing Ideas" anchor chart (AC 1.14):
   - "What should we think about before we make our advertisements?"
   - "Who is our audience?"
   - "What products will we make?"
   - "When will we share our marketing materials?"
   - "Where will we share our products?"
   - "How will we share our products?"

3. Show online examples of town brochures, tourism commercials, and cartoon maps.
4. Instruct learners to fill out a "Planning Sheet" (Appendix B.1). Read directions and answer questions.
5. Assign volunteers to each station to support learners as they work.

Lesson Day 2

1. Pass out the completed "Planning Sheet" worksheet (Appendix B.1) and send learners to their stations.
2. Instruct volunteers to support learners by asking guiding questions.

Lesson Day 3

1. Reflect on progress before going to stations. Ask learners to share the problems they faced. What solutions helped?
2. Assess learning with the "Inquire Create Competencies Rubric" (Appendix A.1).

SHARE LESSON

Objective

Learners will provide constructive feedback on marketing projects.

AASL Standards Framework for Learners: I.C.2. Learners adapt, communicate, and exchange learning products with others in a cycle that includes providing constructive feedback.

> ★ *Create QR codes to access digital projects. Display codes in acrylic sign holders. Connect headphones to laptops and mobile devices for quiet listening.*

Lesson Duration
1 hour

Materials

- Image of a promotional flyer
- Computer or mobile device and projector
- Projects displayed throughout the library
- Directions to access digital projects
- Mobile devices, laptops, and headphones to view digital projects
- "Constructive Feedback" worksheet (WS 1.9); place in piles next to each project
- Pencils
- "Feedback Sentence Starters" anchor chart (AC 1.15)
- "Inquire Share Competencies Rubric" (Appendix A.1)

ANCHOR CHART 1.15

 Feedback Sentence Starters

- » "I like the way you . . . "
- » "My favorite part is . . . "
- » "I think the audience will like . . . "
- » "What do you mean by . . . ?"
- » "Tell me more about . . . "
- » "I am wondering about . . . "
- » "What are your thoughts about . . . ?"

Lesson

1. Ask learners to think about a time when someone gave them advice about a project. Was it helpful? Why did the person offer advice?
2. Give the definition of *constructive feedback*. Explain that today learners will view everyone's marketing products and offer helpful suggestions.
3. Say, "Before we start giving constructive feedback, let's talk about what that looks like and sounds like."
4. Present an image of a promotional flyer. Model how to give feedback with the following sentences:
   - I like the way . . .
   - My favorite part is . . .
   - I wonder if the artist thought about . . .

5. Ask learners what they noticed about the constructive feedback.
6. Write starter sentences together on the "Feedback Sentence Starters" anchor chart (AC 1.15).
7. Give directions about visiting each project and filling out the "Constructive Feedback" worksheet (WS 1.9). Ask learners to begin each "Constructive Feedback" worksheet (WS 1.9) by writing their own name on the paper.
8. Collect the "Constructive Feedback" worksheets (WS 1.9) to assess learning with the "Inquire Share Competencies Rubric" (Appendix A.1).

GROW LESSON

Objective
Learners will finalize their products and invite community members to view their work.

AASL Standards Framework for Learners: I.D.3. Learners participate in an ongoing inquiry-based process by enacting new understanding through real-world connections.

Lesson Duration
2 class sessions, 45–50 minutes each

Materials
- Completed "Constructive Feedback" worksheet (WS 1.9)
- Projects
- Library stations from previous lesson
- "Formal Letter" anchor chart (AC 1.16)
- Lined paper
- Pencils
- "Inquire Grow Competencies Rubric" (Appendix A.1)

Lesson
1. Inform learners that they will read their feedback and finalize their products based on recommendations.
2. Ask learners who they should share their products with once they finish.
3. Tell learners they can write letters and invite town officials and the chamber of commerce to see their products. Officials and chamber members may want to use the projects to promote the town.
4. Ask, "How do we write a formal letter?" Write the format for a formal letter on the "Formal Letter" anchor chart (AC 1.16).

5. Explain that when learners are satisfied with their final products, they can write a letter to a town official or the chamber of commerce.

6. Review letters and final products to assess learning using the "Inquire Grow Competencies Rubric" (Appendix A.1).

Post-Assessment

- Pass out the "Our Town" worksheet (WS 1.8).
- Direct learners to circle the word "Post-Assessment" at the top of the page to distinguish this from the initial assessment.
- Ask learners to respond to the questions.
- Assess learning with the "Inquire Grow Competencies Rubric" (Appendix A.1). Compare responses with the pre-assessment to show growth.

ANCHOR CHART 1.16

🖊 Formal Letter

The Honorable
Mayor of
Street Address
City, State, Zip Code

Dear Mayor _____ :

» Introduce yourself.
» Explain why you are writing the letter.
» Describe what you made and why you made it.
» Add contact information.

Sincerely,

OUR TOWN

Name: _____

Pre-Assessment/Post-Assessment

Why do people live and work in our town?

_____

_____

_____

_____

_____

_____

_____

What would you like to learn about our town?

_____

_____

_____

_____

_____

_____

CONSTRUCTIVE FEEDBACK

Name: _____

Project Name: _____

I like the way you . . .   My favorite part is . . .   I think the audience will like . . .

What do you mean by . . . Tell me more about . . . I am wondering about . . .

What are your thoughts about . . .

_____

_____

_____

- -

CONSTRUCTIVE FEEDBACK

Name: _____

Project Name: _____

I like the way you . . .   My favorite part is . . .   I think the audience will like . . .

What do you mean by . . . Tell me more about . . . I am wondering about . . .

What are your thoughts about . . .

_____

_____

_____

CHAPTER 2

Include Lessons

KEY COMMITMENT
Demonstrate an understanding of and commitment to inclusiveness and respect for diversity in the learning community.

WHAT CAN WE LEARN ABOUT A SOCIETY BY UNDERSTANDING HOW STUDENTS GET TO SCHOOL?

Shared Foundation: Include
Featured Book: *The Way to School*
by Rosemary McCarney

Summary

How do you travel to school? By foot? Car? Taxi? Bus? Subway? How do you think learners in Indonesia, Ghana, and Myanmar get to school? This question is explored with fascinating photographs of students traveling to school. Readers will be amazed at the dangerous journeys learners take to get an education. Compelling images will inspire readers to learn more about the countries in the pictures. Learners will have a new appreciation for school when they compare and contrast journeys from around the world.

Pre-Assessment
- Pass out "The Way to School" worksheet (WS 2.1).
- Ask learners to highlight or circle "Pre-Assessment" at the top of the worksheet.
- Ask learners to write a list of how students from around the world get to school.
- Assess responses using the "Include Create Competencies Rubric" (Appendix A.2).
- Save the results to compare with post-assessments at the end of the unit.

THINK LESSON

Objective
After reading *The Way to School* by Rosemary McCarney, learners will consider why traveling to school is different around the world.

AASL Standards Framework for Learners: II.A.3. Learners contribute a balanced perspective when participating in a learning community by describing their understanding of cultural relevancy and placement within the global learning community.

Lesson Duration
50–60 minutes

Materials
- Copy of *The Way to School* by Rosemary McCarney
- "What Do the Pictures Tell You . . ." anchor chart (AC 2.1)
- Markers
- "Travel to School" worksheet (WS 2.2)
- Pencils
- "Include Think Competencies Rubric" (Appendix A.2)

> ★ *This book will provoke many questions and comments. Ask the collaborating educator to record responses on the "What Do the Pictures Tell You . . ." anchor chart (AC 2.1) while you read the book.*

Lesson
1. Introduce the lesson by asking learners how they get to school. Why do they travel that way? How do they feel about it? Explain that you are going to read a book about how students from around the world travel to school. Tell learners to pay close attention to the pictures in the book. They will gather information and ask questions about what they see. Record responses on the "What Do the Pictures Tell You . . ." anchor chart (AC 2.1).
2. Ask learners what image fascinated them the most. Why does travel look so different in the United States? Tell learners to write their responses on their "Travel to School" worksheets (WS 2.2).
3. Assess the "Travel to School" worksheet (WS 2.2) with the "Include Think Competencies Rubric" (Appendix A.2).

🧭 What Do the Pictures Tell You . . .

Countries	About the Children?	About Where They Live?	About How They Feel?
Philippines	The children are poor. They take care of the way they look. They are brave.	They don't have money to build schools or bridges.	They are not afraid.
Japan	The students look like they take school seriously. They have matching clothes, backpacks, and shoes.	They live where extreme weather destroys buildings.	They look determined to get to school.
United States	The boy has it easy.	He lives where there is money for lunch, cars in the driveway, and school transportation.	He feels comfortable about getting on the bus.
Cambodia	The girls are capable. They have money for uniforms.	There is a lot of water where they live.	They look competent.
Indonesia	They have money for uniforms. They are strong and brave. The girls have to cover their heads, but the man does not.	There are no paved roads in the picture. They don't have money to fix broken bridges.	They look tired and not excited about going to school.
Nepal	The children are brave. They travel without adults.	There are no roads or bridges in the picture.	They don't look scared.
Colombia	The children are courageous.	There are no roads or bridges in the picture.	They seem relaxed.
China	The children know how to be safe. They are brave.	There are no paved roads in the picture.	They look like they are comfortable with heights.
Brazil	They wear regular clothing to school. One girl might not have money for shoes.	They don't have roads or buses.	The children seem indifferent about traveling to school.
Myanmar	The girl looks poor.	There are no roads or cars.	She looks happy.
Canada		There is money to plow the roads.	

⬤ What Do the Pictures Tell You . . . (continued)

Countries	About the Children?	About Where They Live?	About How They Feel?
Ghana	They are used to hard work.	They don't have running water, paved roads, or cars.	They look happy.
Uganda	They are resourceful.	There are no roads.	They look happy.
Tanzania	He has to walk far to get to school.	The road is not paved.	He seems comfortable with walking to school.
Haiti	They have money for uniforms. They enjoy walking together in groups.	The roads are not paved.	They look happy to be together.
Laos	They don't have shoes.	The roads are not paved.	They look nervous.
India	They have to walk far to school.	It is a cold place. Paths are not shoveled or plowed.	They look cold and strong.

CREATE LESSON

Objective
Learners will infer information from different perspectives about the countries named in *The Way to School.*

AASL Standards Framework for Learners: II.B.3. Learners adjust their awareness of the global learning community by representing diverse perspectives during learning activities.

Lesson Duration
50–60 minutes

Materials
- Copy of *The Way to School* by Rosemary McCarney
- Copy of *Brazil* by Colleen Sexton (or another book about Brazil with a school section)
- Copy of *Brazil (My Country)* by Annabel Savery (or another book about Brazil with a school section)
- Map of Brazil
- Books featuring countries mentioned in *The Way to School* by Rosemary McCarney (Brazil, Cambodia, Canada, China, Colombia, Ghana, Haiti, India, Indonesia, Japan, Laos, Myanmar, Nepal, Philippines, Tanzania, Uganda, and United States)
- "What Is the Author Trying to Tell Us about School in Brazil?" anchor chart (AC 2.2)
- Markers
- "Different Representations of a Country" worksheet (WS 2.3)
- Pencils
- "Include Create Competencies Rubric" (Appendix A.2)

> 📌 *This may be a great time to weed your collection! If your country books are more than ten years old, it's time to recycle them.*

Lesson
1. Hold up a copy of *The Way to School.* Ask, "Why do you think Rosemary McCarney wrote this book?"
2. Say, "Let's take a look at the page about Brazil. What do you think the author wants us to know about how students get to school in Brazil?" Write responses on the "What Is the Author Trying to Tell Us about School in Brazil?" anchor chart (AC 2.2).

◐ What Is the Author Trying to Tell Us about School in Brazil?

Book Title	Author's Message
The Way to School by Rosemary McCarney	It's hard to get to school. Children travel in carts made out of twigs with wooden wheels and pulled by an ox. The children do not have supplies—books, backpacks, lunch boxes.
Brazil by Colleen Sexton	The children look happy. They have school supplies. The information states that some children work instead of going to school.
Brazil (My Country) by Annabel Savery	Some children go to school. Others have to work. All children work hard. School is only four hours a day. Children stop going to school when they are 14 years old.

» What can we infer from the different sources of information?

» Some people have money and others are poor. School does not seem to be a priority because school days are short and students graduate when they are 14 years old.

3. Point to a map of Brazil. Say, "Brazil is a large country. I'm wondering if every child in Brazil travels to school the same way. Let's take a look at another book and see what the author wants us to know about school in Brazil."

4. Read two more books that describe Brazilian schools. Ask, "What do the authors want us to learn from their descriptions? What can we infer from the different sources of information?" Write learners' responses on the "What Is the Author Trying to Tell Us about School in Brazil?" anchor chart (AC 2.2).

5. Say, "I wonder what other books have to say about the countries featured in *The Way to School*." Explain that learners will work in groups to study how different authors describe a country. Each group will study one country and fill in the table on the "Different Representations of a Country" worksheet (WS 2.3). Learners will share their information with the class.

6. Collect the worksheets and assess learning with the "Include Create Competencies Rubric" (Appendix A.2).

SHARE LESSON

Objective

After learning how dangerous and arduous it is for some learners to travel to school, learners will discuss why children make the journey and debate whether school is worth the risk.

AASL Standards Framework for Learners: II.C.2. Learners exhibit empathy with and tolerance for diverse ideas by contributing to discussions in which multiple viewpoints on a topic are expressed.

Lesson Duration

2 lessons—1 lesson watching the video (1 hour and 17 minutes) and 1 lesson to discuss viewpoints (50 minutes)

Materials

- *On the Way to School,* an Amazon Prime Video
- "On the Way to School" anchor chart (AC 2.3)
- "Sharing Different Views" anchor chart (AC 2.4)
- Markers
- Sticky notes
- Clipboards
- Pencils
- "Notes for Discussion" worksheet (WS 2.4)
- "Include Share Competencies Rubric" (Appendix A.2)

Lesson Day 1

1. Introduce the lesson by asking learners to think of a morning when it was hard to get to school. What made it difficult? Explain that over the next few classes they will watch a movie about four remarkable students who face incredible challenges on their way to school.
2. Tell learners that as they watch the movie, their job is to respond to what they see by jotting their thoughts on sticky notes. They will write what they wonder about and what they notice. At the end of the video, they will place their sticky notes on the "On the Way to School" anchor chart (AC 2.3). Close the lesson by reading some of the notes aloud.

🔖 On the Way to School

	What Do You Notice?	What Do You Wonder?
Jackson from Kenya		
Samuel from India		
Zahira from Morocco		
Carlos from Argentina		

Sharing Different Views

» State your viewpoint.
» Support your viewpoint with evidence.
» Listen to other viewpoints.
» Consider your thoughts and add to the conversation.

Sentence Starters
» "I agree with what you said and would like to add . . ."
» "That's an interesting point, but I wonder about . . ."
» "I understood it differently. I think . . ."
» "I hear what you are saying, but I disagree because . . ."
» "Would you consider . . . ?"
» "What do you think about . . . ?"
» "I didn't know that. I would like to learn more about . . ."
» "What do you mean by . . . ?"
» "Can you explain more about . . . ?"

Lesson Day 2

1. Introduce the lesson by asking learners to turn and talk with their neighbor about what fascinated them the most about the movie.
2. Pass out the "Notes for Discussion" worksheet (WS 2.4) and ask learners to fill out the first two questions.
3. Prepare learners for discussion by directing their attention to the "Sharing Different Views" anchor chart (AC 2.4).
4. Model what it looks like and sounds like to express a viewpoint. Begin by sharing your views about dogs. Give reasons why you feel the way you do about dogs. Ask the collaborating educator or a library volunteer to disagree with you. Follow the points on the "Sharing Different Views" anchor chart (AC 2.4) to direct the discussion.
5. Ask, "What did you notice about the way we shared our viewpoints?"
6. Explain that learners will share their views about whether the students should take big risks to get to school.
7. Ask learners to wrap up the discussion by responding to the "After Group Discussion" questions on their "Notes for Discussion" worksheet (WS 2.4).
8. Collect the worksheets and assess learning using the "Include Share Competencies Rubric" (Appendix A.2).

GROW LESSON

Objective
Learners will investigate daily activities from around the world to learn more about different societies.

AASL Standards Framework for Learners: II.D.3. Learners demonstrate empathy and equity in knowledge building within the global learning community by reflecting on their own place within the global learning community.

Lesson Duration
50–60 minutes

Materials
- A copy of *This Is How We Do It: One Day in the Lives of Seven Kids from around the World* by Matt Lamothe
- "Gathering Clues" anchor chart (AC 2.5)
- Markers
- "Venn Diagram" (Appendix B.7)
- Pencils
- "Include Grow Competencies Rubric" (Appendix A.2)

ANCHOR CHART 2.5

 Gathering Clues

Country	Make an Inference about the Different Countries
India	It's a busy place with lots of traffic.
Iran	Education is important because children wear tailored uniforms.
Italy	The school hours and trip to school remind me of America.
Japan	Cleanliness is important.
Peru	They don't have money to build sturdy homes.
Russia	Playing sports and board games is part of daily life.
Uganda	It must be hot because the children wear shorts to school and it looks tropical where they live.

*Explore **DK Find Out!**, an AASL Best Website for Teaching and Learning. Click on "Children Just Like Me" to see short video clips from students around the world.*

Lesson

1. Introduce the lesson by asking, "If we were to write a book about what we do every day and send it to another country, what would students learn about us? Today, we are going to read a book about the daily lives of seven students from around the world. While we read the story, gather clues about their communities." Record answers on the "Gathering Clues" anchor chart (AC 2.5).

2. After reading the story, ask the following questions:
   - "What do all of the students have in common?"
   - "What is different?"

3. Tell learners that they will compare their daily activity with the descriptions featured in the book.

4. Pass out the "Venn Diagram" worksheet (Appendix B.7). Direct learners to write their name at the top of the top circle. Write the name of a child featured in the book at the bottom of the bottom circle. If learners share something in common with the child from another country, they will write the similarities where the circles connect. Differences will be designated in the area where the circles do not connect.

5. Assess work with the "Include Grow Competencies Rubric" (Appendix A.2).

Post-Assessment

- Pass out "The Way to School" worksheet (WS 2.1).
- Direct learners to circle the word "Post-Assessment" at the top of the page to distinguish this from the initial assessment.
- Ask learners to respond to the questions.
- Assess learning with the "Include Create Competencies Rubric" (Appendix A.2). Compare responses with the pre-assessment to show growth.

THE WAY TO SCHOOL

Name: _____

Pre-Assessment/Post-Assessment

Directions: Answer the questions below.

How do you get to school?

_____

_____

_____

_____

_____

_____

How would you get to school if you lived in a different country?

_____

_____

_____

_____

_____

_____

TRAVEL TO SCHOOL

Name: _____

What fascinated you the most about the children in *The Way to School*
by Rosemary McCarney?

_____

_____

_____

_____

Why do you think their journey to school is so difficult?

_____

_____

_____

_____

Why is traveling to school so different in the United States?

_____

_____

_____

_____

WORKSHEET 2.3

DIFFERENT REPRESENTATIONS OF A COUNTRY

Name: _____

Directions: Choose a country mentioned in *The Way to School*. Read more books about schools in that country. What do the authors want you to know about the children, their school, and where they live?

Country: _____

Title and Author	What Does the Author Want You to Know?

What can you infer from the different sources of information?

_____

_____

_____

WORKSHEET 2.4

NOTES FOR DISCUSSION

Name: _____

Before Group Discussion

1) Why would the children make the journey?

_____

_____

2) Do you think the children in the movie should take big risks to get to school? Why do you think so?

_____

_____

After Group Discussion

1) Did your thinking change or stay the same after a group discussion?

_____

_____

2) What did you hear that changed your thinking?

_____

_____

3) What did you hear that supported your ideas?

_____

_____

HOW DO PEOPLE DETERMINE WHAT THEY WANT AND WHAT THEY NEED?

Shared Foundation: Include
Featured Book: *I Like, I Don't Like*
by Anna Baccelliere

Summary

Every child on Earth has a right to an education and time
to play. Unfortunately, some children don't have these options. They have to work
in order to eat. The story *I Like, I Don't Like,* by Anna Baccelliere, shows two sides of
childhood: one of privilege and one of poverty. The story follows a simple pattern. One
page features a child enjoying something, while the next page shows another child
working. This thought-provoking story, illustrated with pictures in alluring collage,
will have learners discussing the difference between wants and needs.

Pre-Assessment

- Distribute the "Wants and Needs" worksheet (WS 2.5).
- Ask learners to highlight or circle "Pre-Assessment" at the top of the worksheet.
- Assess responses with the "Include Think Competencies Rubric" (Appendix A.2).
- Save results for a baseline measure.

THINK LESSON

Objective

While reading *I Like, I Don't Like,* learners will interpret why learners from around
the world have different perspectives on toys.

AASL Standards Framework for Learners: II.A.2. Learners contribute a balanced
perspective when participating in a learning community by adopting a discerning
stance toward points of view and opinions expressed in information resources and
learning products.

Lesson Duration

50–60 minutes

Materials

- Copy of *I Like, I Don't Like* by Anna Baccelliere
- "What Do You Notice, What Do You Wonder?" anchor chart (AC 2.6)
- Markers
- "I Like, I Don't Like" worksheet (WS 2.6)
- Pencils
- "Include Think Competencies Rubric" (Appendix A.2)

ANCHOR CHART 2.6

 What Do You Notice, What Do You Wonder?

What Do You Notice?

- » The boy likes shells, toy cars, LEGOs, and soccer.
- » The girl doesn't like rice, bricks, tires, and rugs.
- » The boy who likes bricks is playing with them.
- » The boys who do not like bricks are carrying them on their heads.

What Do You Wonder?

- » I wonder why the girl does not like rugs, tires, bricks, and rice.
- » Why are the man's shoes so large? Why is the girl shining them? Why isn't she wearing shoes?
- » Why are the boys carrying bricks on their heads?

Lesson

1. Pass out the "I Like, I Don't Like" worksheet (WS 2.6). Direct learners to list the things they like in the left-hand column and list the things they don't like in the right-hand column. Explain that they will answer the question at the bottom of the worksheet after they read a story together.

2. Introduce the book *I Like, I Don't Like* by asking learners to look closely at the cover. Ask, "What do you notice? What questions do you have?" Record answers on the "What Do You Notice, What Do You Wonder?" anchor chart (AC 2.6).

3. Read the story. The following question will apply to all pages. Record answers on the "What Do You Notice, What Do You Wonder?" anchor chart (AC 2.6).
   - "What do you notice about these pages? What questions do you have?"

4. Conclude the story by asking learners to think about why the boy on the last page of the book does not know what playing is. Explain that in some parts of the world, children have to work in order to survive. The United Nations tries to help them, but too many children live in poverty.

5. Ask learners to look at their list of things they like and don't like. Has their thinking changed after reading the story?

6. Collect the "I Like, I Don't Like" worksheets (WS 2.6) and assess learning with the "Include Think Competencies Rubric" (Appendix A.2).

CREATE LESSON

Objective

Learners will work in groups to create a list of the six most important things we need to live a fulfilling life.

AASL Standards Framework for Learners: II.B.1. Learners adjust their awareness of the global learning community by interacting with learners who reflect a range of perspectives.

Lesson Duration

40–50 minutes

Materials

- Sticky notes (10 for each student)
- Pencils
- "Sharing Different Views" anchor chart (AC 2.4)
- Markers
- "Group Work Self-Assessment" worksheet (WS 2.7)
- "Include Create Competencies Rubric" (Appendix A.2)

> ★ *Save your anchor charts and display them in your room. The "Sharing Different Views" anchor chart will come in handy during discussions.*

Lesson

1. Ask learners what it means to have a fulfilling life. What do they need to feel satisfied and happy? Learners will write what fulfills them on sticky notes.

2. Explain that they will work together to combine their sticky notes and choose five of the most important things they need to live a fulfilling life.

3. Direct learners' attention to the "Sharing Different Views" anchor chart (AC 2.4). With the collaborating educator, model what it looks like and sounds like

to express a different opinion. Begin by stating an idea and supporting it with details. You may want to use ice cream as an example. State that you need ice cream to live a fulfilling life and explain why. Ask the collaborating educator to disagree with the idea. Follow the sentence starters on the "Sharing Different Views" anchor chart (AC 2.4). Encourage the collaborating educator to state her own idea and discuss it.

4. Ask learners what they noticed about your example.
5. Form small groups of learners. Students will use their sticky notes to share their ideas and listen to contributions. Their job is to agree on five items that they think are essential for living a fulfilling life.
6. Pass out the "Group Work Self-Assessment" worksheet (WS 2.7) and ask learners to answer the questions.
7. Assess responses using the "Include Create Competencies Rubric" (Appendix A.2).

SHARE LESSON

Objective
Learners will compare and contrast the different "Top 5" lists and vote for their favorite list.

AASL Standards Framework for Learners: II.C.1. Learners exhibit empathy with and tolerance for diverse ideas by engaging in informed conversation and active debate.

Lesson Duration
50–60 minutes

Materials
- Poster paper
- Markers
- Crayons
- Sticky notes (from previous lesson and a new stack)
- "Sharing Different Views" anchor chart (AC 2.4)
- "Responding to Different Opinions" worksheet (WS 2.8)
- Pencils
- "Include Share Competencies Rubric" (Appendix A.2)

Lesson

1. Inform learners that today their groups will share their list of the Top 5 most important things for living a fulfilling life. Each group will create a poster that illustrates the students' lists. Groups will present their finished posters.
2. Direct learners' attention to the "Sharing Different Views" anchor chart (AC 2.4). Ask learners to explain what it looks like and sounds like to share different ideas.
3. Tell learners not to worry if they don't have a chance to vocally share an idea about a poster. Their voice will still be heard. You will provide sticky notes for them to write their ideas. They can add their sticky notes to the posters.
4. Pass out the "Responding to Different Opinions" worksheet (WS 2.8). Collect responses to assess learning with the "Include Share Competencies Rubric" (Appendix A.2).

GROW LESSON

Objective

Learners will consider what could make their wants and needs change.

AASL Standards Framework for Learners: II.D.3. Learners demonstrate empathy and equity in knowledge building within the global learning community by reflecting on their own place within the global learning community.

Lesson Duration

45–50 minutes

Materials

- Posters from previous lesson
- Copy of *I Like, I Don't Like* by Anna Baccelliere
- "How Can Wants and Needs Change?" anchor chart (AC 2.7)
- Markers
- Internet access
- Projector
- Access to computers or mobile devices
- "Planning Sheet" worksheet (Appendix B.1)
- "Include Grow Competencies Rubric" (Appendix A.2)

How Can Wants and Needs Change?

- » Job loss
- » Power outage
- » Storm damage
- » Move

How Can We Help?

- » Collect food for the local food bank.
- » Collect school supplies for children in need.
- » Start a book drive for summer vacation.
- » Raise money to help with heating bills.

Lesson

1. Introduce the lesson by inviting learners to share what they know about wants and needs.
2. Ask learners how wants and needs can change. Write responses on the "How Can Wants and Needs Change?" anchor chart (AC 2.7).
3. Review the posters that students made. Hold up a copy of *I Like, I Don't Like* and ask learners to think about the children in the book. What would the children in the book say they need to live a fulfilling life?
4. Inform learners that organizations are working to help children in need. Read about these groups on the last page of the book. The websites mentioned on this page are meant for an older audience. Websites of local food banks and charities might be more appropriate. Brainstorm ideas about how to help. Write ideas on the "How Can Wants and Needs Change?" anchor chart (AC 2.7).
5. Pass out the "Planning Sheet" worksheet (Appendix B.1). Ask learners to write the ideas that intrigued them the most and create a plan to get started helping others.
6. Assess understanding with the "Include Grow Competencies Rubric" (Appendix A.2).

Post-Assessment

- Pass out the "Wants and Needs" worksheet (WS 2.5).
- Direct learners to circle the word "Post-Assessment" at the top of the page to distinguish this from the initial assessment.
- Assess responses with the "Include Think Competencies Rubric" (Appendix A.2).
- Compare results with the pre-assessment.

WANTS AND NEEDS

Name: _____

Pre-Assessment/Post-Assessment

What do children from around the world want?

_____

_____

_____

_____

_____

_____

What do children from around the world need?

_____

_____

_____

_____

_____

_____

_____

I LIKE, I DON'T LIKE

Name: _____

Directions: List the things you like on the left-hand side of the table. List the things you don't like on the right-hand side of the table.

Things I Like	Things I Don't Like
•	•
•	•
•	•
•	•
•	•
•	•
•	•

After reading *I Like, I Don't Like* by Anna Baccelliere, what do you think about the items on your lists?

_____

_____

_____

_____

_____

_____

_____

GROUP WORK SELF-ASSESSMENT

Name: _____

Directions: Respond to each statement by circling "Yes" or "No."

1) I stated my idea.   **YES**   **NO**

2) I supported my idea by giving examples and details.   **YES**   **NO**

3) I listened to my classmates' ideas.   **YES**   **NO**

4) I respectfully added to the conversation.   **YES**   **NO**

5) I used a sentence starter to share my opinion.   **YES**   **NO**

GROUP WORK SELF-ASSESSMENT

Name: _____

Directions: Respond to each statement by circling "Yes" or "No."

1) I stated my idea.   **YES**   **NO**

2) I supported my idea by giving examples and details.   **YES**   **NO**

3) I listened to my classmates' ideas.   **YES**   **NO**

4) I respectfully added to the conversation.   **YES**   **NO**

5) I used a sentence starter to share my opinion.   **YES**   **NO**

RESPONDING TO DIFFERENT OPINIONS

Name: _____

Directions: Respond to the following questions after all groups have shared their "Top 5 List to Live a Fulfilling Life."

What did you hear in the presentations that you agreed with?

_____

_____

_____

What did you disagree with?

_____

_____

_____

How did you express your ideas? Sticky note? Vocally?

_____

_____

_____

How did the presentations change your thinking?

_____

_____

_____

HOW DO PEOPLE DECIDE WHERE TO LIVE?

Shared Foundation: Include
Featured Book: *Why Am I Here?*
by Constance Ørbeck-Nilssen

Summary

Think of where you are right now. What circum-
stances led you to where you live and work? Where
would you be if something in your life was different? *Why Am I Here?*, by Constance
Ørbeck-Nilssen, contemplates these very questions. This philosophical book poet-
ically reveals that children around the world live different lives. How did they end
up where they are? Do they wonder about living somewhere else? The questions are
never answered in the book, but the conclusion tells us that home is wherever you
are in this moment of time. *Why Am I Here?* compels readers to think about how they
ended up where they live today.

Pre-Assessment
- Pass out the "Why Do You Live Here?" worksheet (WS 2.9).
- Ask learners to highlight or circle "Pre-Assessment" at the top of the worksheet.
- Assess responses with the "Include Think Competencies Rubric" (Appendix A.2).
- Save results for a baseline measure.

THINK LESSON

Objective

After reading *Why Am I Here?* by Constance Ørbeck-Nilssen, learners will create a
time line that traces the movements of their ancestors.

AASL Standards Framework for Learners: II.A.3. Learners contribute a balanced
perspective when participating in a learning community by describing their understanding of cultural relevancy and placement within the global learning community.

Lesson Duration
45–50 minutes

Materials

- Copy of *Why Am I Here?* by Constance Ørbeck-Nilssen
- "Why Am I Here?" anchor chart (AC 2.8)
- Markers
- "Interview Questions" worksheet (WS 2.10)
- "Include Think Competencies Rubric" (Appendix A.2)

 Why Am I Here?

What Questions Do You Have?

» What animal is on the cover? Where is the animal from?

» Why is she alone on a rock?

» Why are there homes surrounded by water? Where are the streets? Where is the land?

» Why are they living under the bridge?

» Where do children go when there is a war?

» Why are they traveling to unknown places?

» What are they carrying on their heads?

» Why are children working?

» How do people live in the desert?

Why Do You Think the Author Wrote This Book?

» To help us realize that children around the world live differently.

Lesson

1. Engage learners by asking the following questions:
   - "How many of you have lived in this town since you were a baby?"
   - "How many of you recently moved here?"
   - "Have you ever dreamed of living somewhere else? If so, where would you live?"

2. Explain that today they are going to read a story about someone who wonders about living in different places. Tell learners that as you read the story, you would like to hear their questions. Record questions on the "Why Am I Here?" anchor chart (AC 2.8).

3. Ask the following questions while reading *Why Am I Here?*
   - "What questions do you have about the cover of the book?" (cover)
   - "How is the girl feeling? How can you tell?" (p. 4)

- "What clues can we use on this page to think about the setting?" (p. 6)
- "Why do you think the illustrator used dark colors on this page?" (p. 8)
- "How is the girl feeling on this page? How can you tell?" (p. 10)
- "What questions do you have?" (p. 16)
- "Make a connection with the information on this page." (p. 23)
- "Why do you think the author wrote this story?" (p. 30)

4. Explain that over the next few days, students are going to learn why their families live where they do. They will create a project to tell their stories.
5. Pass out the "Interview Questions" worksheet (WS 2.10). Explain the directions for learners to take home.
6. Assess understanding with the "Include Think Competencies Rubric" (Appendix A.2).

CREATE LESSON

Objective
Learners will work together to create an infographic that shows where they are from and why they live in the town.

AASL Standards Framework for Learners: II.B.1. Learners adjust their awareness of the global learning community by interacting with learners who reflect a range of perspectives.

Lesson Duration
2 lessons, 45–50 minutes each

Materials
- "Group Work" anchor chart (AC 2.9)
- Access to the Internet
- Markers
- Chart paper
- Sticky notes
- Poster paper

Some learners may be sensitive about sharing their family story. Give these students a choice of interviewing a staff member whom they want to learn more about instead.

- Crayons
- Markers
- Completed "Interview Questions" worksheet (WS 2.10)
- "Infographic Group Work Checklist" worksheet (WS 2.11)
- "Include Create Competencies Rubric" (Appendix A.2)

ANCHOR CHART 2.9

 Group Work

What Does Group Work Look Like?

Everyone has a:

» job to do

» turn to talk

» voice to share an opinion or an idea

What Does Group Work Sound Like?

» "What is our goal?"

» "Who is our audience?"

» "What do you think about . . . ?"

» "I like that idea! What do you think, Mary?"

» "Keep going with that idea. I'd like to hear more!"

» "Adding to what you said, what if we . . . ?"

» "Do we all agree?"

» "What changes should we make?"

» "I'm not clear on this idea. Can you explain more?"

Jobs

» **Project Manager:** Keeps the group focused on the goal. Invites everyone to contribute.

» **Timekeeper:** Alerts the group about the remaining time.

» **Illustrator:** Draws the pictures.

» **Presenter:** Describes the final product.

★ *Model the directions for the "Infographic Group Work Checklist" (WS 2.11) with the collaborating educator. Show students what it looks like to create a layout for an infographic with sticky notes. Model how to respectfully discuss and manipulate sticky notes to plan for the infographic.*

Lesson Day 1

1. Ask learners to think about what they discovered during their interviews. Invite students to turn and talk with their neighbor.
2. Explain that they are going to show what they learned by creating an infographic with a group of classmates. Ask, "What is an infographic? Let's see if we can come up with a definition by looking at some examples."
3. Search online for images of infographics. Ask learners what they notice. Write their responses on chart paper. How would they define an infographic?
4. Tell learners that each group will decide how to take everyone's information and display it in an infographic. Ask, "How can we work together as a team to make sure every voice is heard while creating an infographic?" Discuss what teamwork looks like and sounds like. List the roles learners can take while working on a project together. Record ideas on the "Group Work" anchor chart (AC 2.9).
5. Direct learners to begin group work by sharing what they learned from their interviews. Next, they will sketch some ideas on a sticky note based on what they heard. Then, learners will discuss the ideas and think about how to include everyone's story on one infographic.
6. Form groups of learners. Pass out the "Infographic Group Work Checklist" worksheets (WS 2.11), sticky notes, and pencils.

Lesson Day 2

1. Ask learners to share what went well with their group work. Discuss how they solved problems.
2. Tell learners they will create their final infographic today.
3. End the session by asking groups to share their infographics.
4. Review infographics and the "Infographic Group Work Checklist" to assess learning with the "Include Create Competencies Rubric" (Appendix A.2).
5. Display infographics in the library.

SHARE LESSON

Objective

Learners will work together to advertise the best place to live.

AASL Standards Framework for Learners: II.C.1. Learners exhibit empathy with and tolerance for diverse ideas by engaging in informed conversation and active debate.

Lesson Duration

50 minutes

Materials

- Sticky notes
- Pencils
- "Agreeing and Disagreeing" anchor chart (AC 2.10)
- Library books from the geography and travel collection
- "The Perfect Place to Live Checklist" worksheet (WS 2.12)
- "Include Share Competencies Rubric" (Appendix A.2)

ANCHOR CHART 2.10

 Agreeing and Disagreeing

What Does It Look Like?

- » Look at the person who is talking.
- » Give the person time to make her or his point.
- » Add your own ideas.
- » Give supporting details.

What Does It Sound Like?

- » "That's an interesting idea. I'd like to learn more about that."
- » "I see you feel strongly about that. Would you consider thinking about . . . ?"
- » "I heard you say. . . . Is that what you meant?"
- » "Tell me more about why you feel that way."
- » "Great points. I'd like to add . . ."
- » "This is what I'm thinking. . . . What are your thoughts?"

★ *Spend time modeling what it looks like and sounds like to agree and disagree. If a collaborating educator is not available, invite another stakeholder to help.*

Lesson

1. Introduce the lesson by asking learners to think of a favorite place. Where is it? What do they like about it? Explain that they will work with their group to decide where the best place to live is.

2. Model what it looks like and sounds like to share ideas. Ask the collaborating educator to join you. Name a place where you would want to live. Give reasons why you want to live there. Ask the collaborating educator to share his favorite place and explain why he wants to live there. Try to convince one another to agree on the best place to live. Model how to agree and disagree with ideas until a final decision is made. Ask learners what they noticed. Write their responses on the "Agreeing and Disagreeing" anchor chart (AC 2.10).

3. Tell learners it is their turn to work as a group to decide where the best place is to live. First, they will share their own ideas and explain their choices. Then, they will listen to other ideas. Learners are invited to look at books to help them support their argument and research the location. Finally, they will agree on a place and explain their reasoning to the class.

4. Pass out "The Perfect Place to Live Checklist" worksheet (WS 2.12). Read directions and check for understanding.

5. Invite learners to share their final choice and explain how they arrived at that conclusion.

6. Assess final work with the "Include Share Competencies Rubric" (Appendix A.2).

GROW LESSON

Objective

Learners will reflect on ideas they would like to spend time exploring.

AASL Standards Framework for Learners: II.D.2. Learners demonstrate empathy and equity in knowledge building within the global learning community by demonstrating interest in other perspectives during learning activities.

Lesson Duration

45–50 minutes

Materials

- Computer lab or mobile devices
- Access to library databases and geography books
- *Google Maps Street View Treks,* an **AASL Best Website for Teaching and Learning**
- "Ideas I Want to Explore" anchor chart (AC 2.11)
- "I Wonder, I Learned" worksheet (WS 2.13)
- "Include Grow Competencies Rubric" (Appendix A.2)

Lesson

1. Ask learners to share interesting ideas they have heard over the past few days. What would they like to spend time learning more about? Record responses on the "Ideas I Want to Explore" anchor chart (AC 2.11).
2. Pass out the "I Wonder, I Learned" worksheet (WS 2.13). Explain that students will find answers to their questions by searching the library databases, geography and travel books, and *Google Maps Street View Treks.*
3. Assess work with the "Include Grow Competencies Rubric" (Appendix A.2).

Post-Assessment

- Pass out the "Why Do You Live Here?" worksheet (WS 2.9).
- Direct learners to circle the word "Post-Assessment" at the top of the page to distinguish this from the initial assessment.
- Assess responses with the "Include Think Competencies Rubric" (Appendix A.2).
- Compare results with the pre-assessment.

Ideas I Want to Explore

I wonder
what it would be
like to live in . . .

_____

_____

_____

_____

_____

I want to
learn more about . . .

_____

_____

_____

_____

I wonder why . . .

_____

_____

_____

_____

WORKSHEET 2.9

WHY DO YOU LIVE HERE?

Name: _____

Pre-Assessment/Post-Assessment

Name of town: _____

Why do you live here?

_____

_____

_____

_____

_____

_____

_____

_____

_____

_____

_____

_____

_____

_____

INTERVIEW QUESTIONS

Name: _____

Directions: Interview a parent, a grandparent, or a guardian to learn why you live where you do. Ask the following questions and record the person's answers. At the bottom of the worksheet, summarize why you are here.

WHO lived with you when you moved to this town? _____

_____

WHAT was it about the town that made you want to move here? ___

_____

WHEN did I move here? _____

_____

WHY did we move here? _____

_____

WHERE did we live before? _____

_____

HOW did you find our home? _____

_____

. . . .

Summarize: Why are you here? _____

_____

INFOGRAPHIC GROUP WORK CHECKLIST

Name: _____

- ☐ Read the responses from your "Interview Questions" worksheet with the group.
- ☐ Listen to others read their interview work.
- ☐ Think about how you can represent everyone's story on one infographic.
- ☐ Sketch an idea for the infographic on a sticky note.
- ☐ Listen to everyone's ideas.
- ☐ Place sticky notes on the poster paper to plan the final infographic.
- ☐ Draw your infographic.

THE PERFECT PLACE TO LIVE CHECKLIST

Name: _____

- ☐ Tell your group where you want to live.
- ☐ Give three reasons why you want to live there.
- ☐ Share your reasoning with the group.
- ☐ Listen to other ideas.

Ideas I agreed with:

_____

_____

_____

_____

_____

Ideas I disagreed with:

_____

_____

_____

_____

_____

I WONDER, I LEARNED

Name:

Directions: Complete the sentences in the table below.

I Wonder . . .	I Learned . . .

WHAT DO STATUES REPRESENT?

Shared Foundation: Include
Featured Book: *Her Right Foot* by David Eggers

Summary

Did you know the Statue of Liberty was not always green? It's true! Lady Liberty was originally brown, but her copper covering weathered over time and changed color. Dave Eggers, the author of *Her Right Foot,* informs the reader about the statue in a conversational manner. You can almost hear his voice as he poses questions and prompts you to answer them. Engaging illustrations will also intrigue readers. Shadows peeking from under shapes make figures appear to be floating above the page. The end of the story asks readers to think about what the Statue of Liberty represents. They'll realize Lady Liberty is so much more than a statue. This lesson guides learners to create a statue that represents classroom values.

Pre-Assessment

- Pass out "The Statue of Liberty" worksheet (WS 2.14).
- Ask learners to highlight or circle "Pre-Assessment" at the top of the worksheet.
- Tell learners to write about what the Statue of Liberty means to them.
- Assess background knowledge with the "Include Think Competencies Rubric" (Appendix A.2).

THINK LESSON

Objective

Learners will consider what the Statue of Liberty represents while reading *Her Right Foot* by Dave Eggers.

AASL Standards Framework for Learners: II.A.2. Learners contribute a balanced perspective when participating in a learning community by adopting a discerning stance toward points of view and opinions expressed in information resources and learning products.

Lesson Duration

2 lessons, 45–50 minutes each

Materials
- "Tracking Our Thinking" anchor chart (AC 2.12)
- Markers
- Sticky notes
- Pencils
- "Opinion" worksheet (Appendix B.9)
- "Include Think Competencies Rubric" (Appendix A.2)

Lesson Day 1

1. Introduce the lesson by showing learners the picture of the Statue of Liberty found at the end of the book. Ask, "How many of you know about this statue? What do you know?"
2. Say, "This is a book about the Statue of Liberty. One idea I would like us all to think about as I read *Her Right Foot* is what the Statue of Liberty represents."
3. Ask the following questions as you read the story and record responses on the "Tracking Our Thinking" anchor chart (AC 2.12):
   - "Read the title and look at the illustration. What questions do you have?" (cover)
   - "What have we learned so far?" (pp. 9–10)
   - "What questions do you have?" (p. 11)
   - "What did you learn about how they built the statue?" (p. 24)
   - "What did you learn on this page? Why is it important?" (p. 31) *America is not ruled by another country.*
   - "Why do you think her crown represents the seven oceans and the seven continents?" (p. 33) *Anyone from around the world is welcome in America.*
   - "What does the torch symbolize? Why is that important to know?" (p. 35) *People can live freely in America.*
   - "Why do you think there are no illustrations on these pages?" (pp. 43–44) *The author wants to make a point.*
   - "Where do you think she is going?" (p. 75)
   - "What questions do you have?" (p. 79)
   - "What is the author trying to tell us?" (pp. 82–93)

4. Invite learners to think about what the Statue of Liberty represents. Ask learners to define the word *immigrants.*
5. Ask, "Should America continue to welcome immigrants? Write your answer on a sticky note. Jot down one to three ideas noting why or why not. Please write your name and place the sticky note on the "Tracking Our Thinking" anchor chart (AC 2.12) under the proper heading. Tomorrow, we will discuss your answers."

⬤ Tracking Our Thinking

I Wonder . . .	I Learned . . .
» Why is the book about her right foot? » Why did the French give America such a big gift? Who paid for the Statue of Liberty? » Why did they use copper? » Why did they make the statue so big? » Why did they keep the statue up for a year in France? » How did they decide to symbolize the seven seas and seven continents? » What are immigrants? » What does the word *symbol* mean? » Why was she chained? » What does the word oppression mean?	» French people wanted to build a statue for America as a gift. » They built the statue in France, took it apart, and shipped it to America. » The Statue of Liberty is holding a book with the year America declared independence. » Her crown represents the seven seas and the seven continents. » The torch lights the way to liberty and freedom. » The Statue of Liberty is always working to welcome people from around the world.

Do you think America should continue to welcome immigrants?   **YES   NO**
Why or why not? Please jot down one to three ideas to support your reasoning.

_____

_____

_____

_____

Lesson Day 2

1. Ask learners to explain what the Statue of Liberty represents.
2. Explain that today they will discuss their ideas about whether America should allow immigrants in the country.
3. Begin by asking a volunteer to read her sticky note. Does everyone agree? If not, why? What is their reasoning?
4. Continue in this fashion, prompting and modeling what it sounds like to respectfully disagree.
5. Ask learners if the discussion changed their mind. Pass out the "Opinion" worksheet (Appendix B.9).
6. Assess learning by considering responses with the "Include Think Competencies Rubric" (Appendix A.2).

CREATE LESSON

Objective

Learners will work together to design a statue for their classroom.

AASL Standards Framework for Learners: II.B.1. Learners adjust their awareness of the global learning community by interacting with learners who reflect a range of perspectives.

Lesson Duration

45–50 minutes

Materials

- "Our Class Values" anchor chart (AC 2.13)
- Markers
- "Statue Design" worksheet (WS 2.15)
- "Include Create Competencies Rubric" (Appendix A.2)
- Poster paper
- Crayons
- Markers
- Pencils

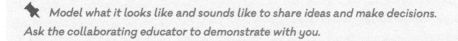

Model what it looks like and sounds like to share ideas and make decisions. Ask the collaborating educator to demonstrate with you.

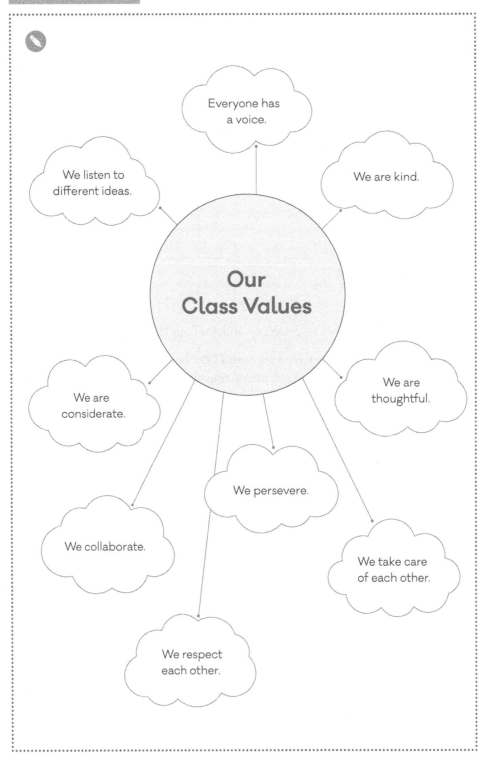

Lesson

1. Introduce the lesson by asking students what they learned about the Statue of Liberty. What does she symbolize? What do they remember about her crown, the torch, and the book she holds?
2. Explain that learners will work in groups to design a statue that represents their classroom values. What are their values? Brainstorm ideas and record them on the "Our Class Values" anchor chart (AC 2.13).
3. Direct learners to work together to design a statue. First, they will discuss ideas. Then, each student will draw a quick sketch of his idea. Next, the group will review all sketches and consider combining the ideas they like to make one statue.
4. Pass out the "Statue Design" worksheet (WS 2.15). Learners will draw their final group design on poster paper and give their statue a title.
5. Assess skill development with the "Include Create Competencies Rubric" (Appendix A.2).

SHARE LESSON

Objective

Learners will explain the different aspects of their statues and explain why their statue should be considered to represent their class.

AASL Standards Framework for Learners: II.C.2. Learners exhibit empathy with and tolerance for diverse ideas by contributing to discussions in which multiple viewpoints on a topic are expressed.

Lesson Duration

45 minutes

Materials

- Posters from previous lesson
- "Statue Presentations" anchor chart (AC 2.14)
- Markers
- Pieces of scrap paper
- Pencils
- "Responding to Ideas" worksheet (WS 2.16)
- "Include Share Competencies Rubric" (Appendix A.2)

Statue Presentations

Group 1: Title of Statue
Ideas and comments from the audience:

»

»

»

Group 2: Title of Statue
Ideas and comments from the audience:

»

»

»

Group 3: Title of Statue
Ideas and comments from the audience:

»

»

»

Group 4: Title of Statue
Ideas and comments from the audience:

»

»

»

Lesson

1. Tell learners that today they will present their design to the class. Write the title of each statue on the "Statue Presentations" anchor chart (AC 2.14). Encourage the audience to ask questions and comment on designs. They will vote for their favorite design after the presentations.
2. Pass out pieces of scrap paper and ask learners to write the title of their favorite poster.
3. Tally the votes and announce the winning design.
4. Pass out the "Responding to Ideas" worksheet (WS 2.16) for reflection.
5. Assess skill development with the "Include Share Competencies Rubric" (Appendix A.2).

GROW LESSON

Objective

Learners will work together as a team to build the classroom statue.

AASL Standards Framework for Learners: II.D.2. Learners demonstrate empathy and equity in knowledge building within the global learning community by demonstrating interest in other perspectives during learning activities.

Lesson Duration

2 lessons—one 50- to 60-minute lesson for building statues and a shorter lesson for reflection

> ★ *Collaborate with the art teacher for this lesson. The art teacher will have valuable insight, and learners will love seeing this educator in the library.*

Materials

- "Ideas I Heard" anchor chart (AC 2.15)
- Markers
- "Statue Description" worksheet (WS 2.17)
- Pencils
- Library maker stations set up ahead of time:
  - Playdough station
  - LEGO station
  - Aluminum foil station
  - Recycled materials station with glue, tape, and scissors
- "Include Grow Competencies Rubric" (Appendix A.2)

◐ Ideas I Heard

I liked [   ] 's idea about . . .

_____

_____

My favorite part of the statue is . . .

_____

_____

The most interesting detail was the . . .

_____

_____

Lesson Day 1

1. Tell learners that they will create their own statue based on all the different ideas they heard over the past few days. What ideas caught their attention? Write them on the "Ideas I Heard" anchor chart (AC 2.15).

2. Describe the different maker stations. Tell students to think about how they can use the materials at each station to build their statue. Assign learners to stations by pulling students' names from a jar. Stations will close once they are full.

Lesson Day 2

1. Tell learners that you saw many ideas represented in the statues they built. Today, they are going to think about what ideas influenced their designs.

2. Distribute the "Statue Description" worksheet (WS 2.17).

3. Assess learning with the "Include Grow Competencies Rubric" (Appendix A.2).

INCLUDE LESSONS | **93**

Post-Assessment

- Pass out the "The Statue of Liberty" worksheet (WS 2.14).
- Direct learners to circle the word "Post-Assessment" at the top of the page to distinguish this from the initial assessment.
- Tell learners to write about what the Statue of Liberty means to them.
- Assess background knowledge with the "Include Think Competencies Rubric" (Appendix A.2).

THE STATUE OF LIBERTY

Name: _____

Pre-Assessment/Post-Assessment

Directions: What does the Statue of Liberty mean to you? Write your answer below.

_____

_____

_____

_____

_____

_____

_____

_____

_____

_____

_____

_____

WORKSHEET 2.15

STATUE DESIGN

Name: _____

Directions: Your group will design a statue that represents your class values. Follow the tasks below to create a group statue. Check off each box when the job is complete.

- ☐ What ideas do you have for the statue? Share them with the group.

- ☐ What ideas do others have? Note the ideas that interest you.

> Draw a quick sketch of a statue that captures the ideas you heard.

- ☐ Share your sketch with the group. Explain your ideas.

Look at other sketches. What ideas should the group keep?

_____

_____

_____

RESPONDING TO IDEAS

Name: _____

Directions: Answer the questions below.

> What does it look like to listen to someone's ideas?

What does it sound like to listen to someone's ideas?

_____

_____

> What does it look like to agree or disagree with an idea?

What does it sound like to agree or disagree with an idea?

_____

_____

STATUE DESCRIPTION

Name: _____

Describe your statue:

_____

_____

_____

_____

_____

_____

How did you incorporate your classmates' ideas in your design?

_____

_____

_____

_____

_____

_____

CHAPTER 3

Collaborate Lessons

KEY COMMITMENT
Work effectively with others to broaden perspectives and work toward common goals.

WHAT MAKES A TEAM SUCCESSFUL?

Shared Foundation: Collaboration
Featured Book: *How to Build a Plane:
A Soaring Adventure of Mechanics, Teamwork,
and Friendship* by Saskia Lacey

Summary

Have you ever had an idea to build something really cool? Did you share your idea with friends and ask them to help? In *How to Build a Plane* by Saskia Lacey, we meet Eli, who is a dreamer. He relies on his friends' talents to help him build a plane. One friend has a flair for research, while another is an expert at putting things together. Children will enjoy seeing the design process in action through Eli's work. Labels, captions, and diagrams help tell the story. Put this book on the lap of an aeronautic enthusiast, and she will pore over the informative pages. When reading to an audience, the first twenty pages are perfect for illustrating the design process. Read these pages to inspire teams to create a paper airplane that soars.

Pre-Assessment

- Distribute the "Teamwork Assessment" worksheet (WS 3.1).
- Ask learners to highlight or circle "Pre-Assessment" at the top of the worksheet.
- Direct learners to answer the questions on the worksheet.
- Assess skill development with the "Collaborate Think Competencies Rubric" (Appendix A.3).

THINK LESSON

Objective

After reading *How to Build a Plane: A Soaring Adventure of Mechanics, Teamwork, and Friendship,* learners will develop a plan to work together to design a paper airplane.

AASL Standards Framework for Learners: III.A.3. Learners identify collaborative opportunities by deciding to solve problems informed by group interaction.

Lesson Duration

60 minutes

Materials

- Copy of *How to Build a Plane: A Soaring Adventure of Mechanics, Teamwork, and Friendship* by Saskia Lacey
- "Teamwork" anchor chart (AC 3.1)
- Markers
- "Teamwork Checklist" worksheet (WS 3.2)
- Drawing paper
- Paper airplane books
- Access to the Internet
- Projector
- *Wonderopolis: How Far Can a Paper Airplane Fly?,* an **AASL Best Website for Teaching and Learning**
- Pencils
- "Collaborate Think Competencies Rubric" (Appendix A.3)

ANCHOR CHART 3.1

🚫 Teamwork

- » The mice are building the wing of the plane together.
- » The mice are looking at a diagram of a plane.
- » Each character has a job title.
- » Phoebe offers to help and begins to search for helpful information.
- » Phoebe and Eli discuss ideas and compromise.
- » Hank offers to help.
- » They make a plan.
- » They test their plane.

There are plenty of online videos showing birds in flight. The slow-motion videos are ideal for this lesson.

Lesson

1. Introduce the lesson by reading the book title and asking learners what they know about teamwork. Explain that while you read the story, their job is to point out examples of teamwork. Write responses on the "Teamwork" anchor chart (AC 3.1).

2. Ask the following questions while reading the book:
   - "What is happening on the cover of the book?"
   - "What do you notice on this page?" (title page)
   - "What do you notice about the titles under the characters' names?" (pp. 6–7)
   - "What is happening in this illustration?" (p. 8)
   - "What happens when Eli's friends help him with his projects?" (p. 9)
   - "Why is Phoebe's question important?" (p. 12)
   - "What is happening on this page?" (p. 16)
   - "Why are plans important?" (p. 17)
   - "What is happening on these pages?" (pp. 18–19)

3. Stop reading at the end of page 19. The beginning of the book is perfect for the general audience, while the rest is best for airplane enthusiasts.

4. Remind learners that Phoebe asked if the wings of a plane work like the wings of a bird. Watch a slow-motion video of birds in flight to consider her question. Show a picture of an airplane and compare it to a picture of a bird. What is the same? What is different?

5. Explain that today learners will work with a team to design a paper airplane.

6. Show learners different paper airplane designs found on *Wonderopolis*. Visit the *How Far Can a Paper Airplane Fly?* page and find tutorials at the end of the post.

7. Pass out one "Teamwork Checklist" worksheet (WS 3.2) for each team.

8. Assess Competencies with the "Collaborate Think Competencies Rubric" (Appendix A.3).

CREATE LESSON

Objective

Learners will work together to make paper airplanes and run test flights.

AASL Standards Framework for Learners: III.B.2. Learners participate in personal, social, and intellectual networks by establishing connections with other learners to build on their own prior knowledge and create new knowledge.

Lesson Duration

45–50 minutes

Materials

- Internet access and projector to view *Inspiration Video* on the *Curiosity Machine* website (the web address is located in the "Online Resources" section at the end of the book)
- Paper
- Tape
- Scissors
- Paper airplane books
- "Test Flight" worksheet (WS 3.3)
- Pencils
- "Bird Wings KWL Chart" anchor chart (AC 3.2)
- Measuring tape
- "Collaborate Create Competencies Rubric" (Appendix A.3)

ANCHOR CHART 3.2

 Bird Wings KWL Chart

I Know . . .	I Wonder . . .	I Learned . . .
» that birds use wings to fly » that wings have feathers » some birds migrate	» about different wing shapes » feathers help birds fly » how far they fly	» that birds with longer wings can travel far

Lesson

1. Ask learners to share what they grasped about teamwork while designing their paper airplanes. Explain that they will work with their groups to make the paper airplanes. Ask, "What do you think your paper airplane will need to travel far?"

2. Watch *Inspiration Video* to learn how the length of wings determines how far a bird can fly. Ask, "What did you learn about the length of wings?" Write answers on the "Bird Wings KWL Chart" anchor chart (AC 3.2).

3. Direct learners to apply their new understandings of flight to help them make paper airplanes. Pass out the "Test Flight" worksheet (WS 3.3). Explain that learners will test their designs and measure how far the paper airplanes fly. Encourage learners to make adaptations along the way. Invite them to talk with other groups to solve problems and generate ideas. Ask guiding questions while learners work through the design process.

4. Collect worksheets and assess learning with the "Collaborate Create Competencies Rubric" (Appendix A.3).

 ## SHARE LESSON

Objective

Learners will work together to create a how-to presentation for a "Paper Airplane Maker Space."

AASL Standards Framework for Learners: III.C.1. Learners work productively with others to solve problems by soliciting and responding to feedback from others.

Lesson Duration

3 lessons, 60 minutes each

> ★ *If learners are not familiar with e-book–creating apps or with video recording equipment, spend a lesson introducing the tools and devices.*

Materials

- Library centers set up ahead of time:
  - Mobile devices with an e-book creator app and paper
  - Video recording equipment and paper
  - Poster board, markers, crayons, glue, and paper

- "How-To Presentations" anchor chart (AC 3.3)
- Markers
- "Presentation Plan" worksheet (WS 3.4)
- Sticky notes

- Pencils
- "Feedback Exit Slip" (WS 3.5)
- "Collaborate Share Competencies Rubric" (Appendix A.3)

ANCHOR CHART 3.3

 How-To Presentations

What makes a good how-to video?

» Close-up shots

» Still camera

» Loud, clear voice

» Clear directions

What makes a good how-to e-book?

» Close-up shots

» Clear pictures

» Easy-to-follow steps with numbers or bullet points

» Labels

» Diagrams

» Clear directions

What makes a good how-to poster?

» Limited amount of words

» Clear, direct steps

» Labels

» Diagrams

Lesson Day 1

1. Ask learners to raise their hands if they have visited a museum. Continue the conversation by asking the following questions:
   - "Did the museum have stations where visitors could make something?"
   - "What did you make?"
   - "How did you know what to do once you were at the station?"

2. Explain that learners are going to make a presentation demonstrating how to build a paper airplane. This presentation will be part of a "Paper Airplane Maker Space" that they will donate to classrooms. The presentation can be a poster, a movie, or an e-book.

3. Ask learners what they should think about when making a how-to presentation. Write responses on the "How-To Presentations" anchor chart (AC 3.3).

4. Explain that learners will work in groups for this project. Before they get to work, they must meet with their group to plan their project.

5. Pass out sticky notes. Instruct learners to illustrate an idea they have for a presentation. Explain that learners will share their ideas with their group during the next class session. Ask learners to put their names on their sticky notes. Gather each group's notes together and save them for the next class session.

Lesson Day 2

1. Distribute one "Presentation Plan" worksheet to each group (WS 3.4).
2. Pass out the sticky notes from the previous lesson.
3. Ask learners to share their ideas and agree on one presentation plan. Once a plan is set in place, learners will fill out the "Presentation Plan" worksheet (WS 3.4) and begin creating.

Lesson Day 3

1. When projects are finished, learners will present their work to classmates. Explain that they will ask for feedback from the audience after they are done presenting. Point to the "How-To Presentations" anchor chart (AC 3.3) to remind students what to look for in a presentation. Give learners time to make improvements.
2. Distribute the "Feedback Exit Slip" worksheet (WS 3.5). Ask learners to respond to the questions.
3. Assess proficiency with the "Collaborate Share Competencies Rubric" (Appendix A.3).

GROW LESSON

Objective

Learners will reflect on their experiences with teamwork.

AASL Standards Framework for Learners: III.D.2. Learners actively participate with others in learning situations by recognizing learning as a social responsibility.

Lesson Duration

45–50 minutes

Materials

- "Collaboration" anchor chart (AC 3.4)
- Markers
- "Teamwork Reflection" worksheet (WS 3.6)
- "Teamwork Assessment" worksheet (WS 3.1)
- "Collaborate Grow Competencies Rubric" (Appendix A.3)

Collaboration

Advantages	Disadvantages
» People help do the work. » Everyone has a job. » People share different ideas and opinions. » Projects are more fun when friends help.	» You may end up doing all the work if classmates don't want to help. » You may not agree with other ideas or opinions. » Some people do all the work because they want things done their way.

Lesson

1. Ask learners to remember what Eli, the mouse in the book, said he needed to build his dream. Say, "Yes, he needed help from his friends! They each had a job, and they helped him build a plane." Remind learners that they worked with their classmates to design a paper airplane that could fly a great distance. They also collaborated to create how-to presentations.

2. Ask, "What were the benefits of working together? What were the disadvantages? If you had to do the projects over again, would you want to work with the same team? Why or why not?" Write responses on the "Collaboration" anchor chart (AC 3.4).

3. Pass out the "Teamwork Reflection" worksheet (WS 3.6).

4. Assess answers by using the "Collaborate Grow Competencies Rubric" (Appendix A.3).

Post-Assessment

- Distribute the "Teamwork Assessment" worksheet (WS 3.1).
- Direct learners to circle the word "Post-Assessment" at the top of the page to distinguish this from the initial assessment.
- Ask learners to answer the questions on the worksheet.
- Assess growth with the "Collaborate Think Competencies Rubric" (Appendix A.3).

TEAMWORK ASSESSMENT

Name: _____

Pre-Assessment/Post-Assessment

What does teamwork look like? Draw a picture in the box below.

What important roles do team members have?

- _____ - _____

- _____ - _____

- _____ - _____

When a team runs into problems, what should team members do?

_____

_____

_____

TEAMWORK CHECKLIST

Names of Team Members:

- _____   • _____

- _____   • _____

- _____   • _____

Directions: Work together to design a paper airplane that will fly. You have thirty minutes to complete the tasks listed below.

☐ Assign a job to everyone in your group. Write the person's name after each job title.

Dreamer: _____

Expert: _____

Illustrator: _____

Project Manager: _____

☐ The **Dreamer** will share ideas.

☐ The **Expert** will research how to make a paper airplane and share it with the group.

☐ The **Illustrator** will draw a sketch of a paper airplane based on information shared by the Dreamer and the Expert.

☐ The **Project Manager** will keep track of time and make sure everyone is staying on task and has what he or she needs.

Draw the team's paper airplane design in the box below.

TEST FLIGHT

Name: _____

Directions: Fly your paper airplane. Measure how far it flies. How can you make it go farther?

Test 1

How far did your plane fly? _____

How can you make it go farther? _____

Test 2

How far did your plane fly? _____

How can you make it go farther? _____

Test 3

How far did your plane fly? _____

How can you make it go farther? _____

Who did you talk to about your design process? _____

_____

Did they help you? How so? _____

_____

Did you offer help? How did you help? _____

_____

PRESENTATION PLAN

Name: _____

Names of Team Members and their job title:

1) _____

2) _____

3) _____

4) _____

Are you creating a movie or an e-book? Draw pictures of what each scene will look like in the storyboard below.

Are you designing a poster board? Draw your idea on the back of this paper.

FEEDBACK EXIT SLIP

Name: _____

What feedback did you offer to another group?

_____

_____

_____

_____

What feedback did another group give you?

_____

_____

_____

_____

What changes did you make to your presentation based on feedback?

_____

_____

_____

_____

TEAMWORK REFLECTION

Name: _____

Directions: Answer the questions below.

1) What went well during your teamwork projects?

_____

_____

_____

2) What problems did you work through?

_____

_____

_____

3) What did you learn about teamwork?

_____

_____

_____

4) Why is good teamwork important?

_____

_____

_____

HOW CAN LISTENING TO IDEAS HELP US DEVELOP A SUCCESSFUL PLAN?

Shared Foundation: Collaboration
Featured Book: *Shh! We Have a Plan*
by Chris Haughton

Summary

Did you ever notice that often the best ideas come from the quietest person in the room? Author Chris Haughton draws attention to this observation in *Shh! We Have a Plan.* Spare text and entertaining illustrations tell a slapstick story about listening to ideas. Readers will enjoy the predictable scenario that will keep them smiling and giggling. Haughton leaves the story open-ended, welcoming learners to write another chapter.

Pre-Assessment

- Pass out the "Making a Plan" worksheet (WS 3.7).
- Read the directions with learners.
- Ask learners to highlight or circle "Pre-Assessment" at the top of the worksheet.
- Assess responses with the "Collaborate Share Competencies Rubric" (Appendix A.3).

THINK LESSON

Objective

After reading *Shh! We Have a Plan* by Chris Haughton, learners will collaborate on a plan to capture a squirrel.

AASL Standards Framework for Learners: III.A.3. Learners identify collaborative opportunities by deciding to solve problems informed by group interaction.

Lesson Duration

50 minutes

Materials

- Copy of *Shh! We Have a Plan* by Chris Haughton
- "Group Interaction" anchor chart (AC 3.5)
- Markers

- "Squirrel Catching Plan" (WS 3.8)
- Pencils
- "Collaborate Think Competencies Rubric" (Appendix A.3)

 Group Interaction

Tips for Discussing a Plan with a Group
- » Give everyone a chance to talk.
- » Ask quiet members to share their thoughts.
- » Discuss all ideas.
- » Agree to try the most popular plan.
- » Follow the plan.
- » Reflect to make improvements.

★ *Offer sticky notes and drawing supplies for learners who are uncomfortable with sharing their ideas aloud. Some learners may need time to reflect on other ideas before contributing.*

Lesson

1. Introduce the book by reading the title and asking learners to think about the people on the cover. Ask, "What is their body language telling us? What do you suppose the smallest person is thinking?"
2. As you read the story, ask the following questions:
   - "What do you notice about the smallest character?" (cover)
   - "What do you think the plan is?" (pp. 1–2)
   - "What can you infer about the smallest character in the story?" (pp. 1–8)
   - "What do you notice about how they make a plan?" (pp. 9–10)
   - "Why do you think the big characters in the story always 'shush' the little character?" (p. 16)
   - "What is happening on these pages?" (pp. 23–24)
   - "What do you predict will happen next?" (p. 37)

3. Conclude the story by asking learners why it's important to listen to everyone's ideas when making a plan.

4. Ask, "What tips would you give the characters in the book about working together to create a plan?" Write the tips on the "Group Interaction" anchor chart (AC 3.5).

5. Explain that learners are going to help the characters catch the squirrel that got away at the end of the story. Learners will work in groups to develop the plan. First, they will discuss ideas and agree on a plan. Then, one member of the group will write the plan.

6. Pass out one "Squirrel Catching Plan" worksheet (WS 3.8) to each group.

7. Assess learning with the "Collaborate Think Competencies Rubric" (Appendix A.3).

CREATE LESSON

Objective
Learners will illustrate a page for *Shh! We Have a Plan* and share it on a collaborative workspace.

AASL Standards Framework for Learners: III.B.2. Learners participate in personal, social, and intellectual networks by establishing connections with other learners to build on their own prior knowledge and create new knowledge.

Lesson Duration
2 lessons, 45–50 minutes each

Materials
- Copy of *Shh! We Have a Plan* by Chris Haughton
- Construction paper (blue, purple, black, white, orange, and pink)
- Scissors
- Glue
- Computer lab or mobile devices
- "Noticing Illustrations" anchor chart (AC 3.6)
- "Group Illustration" worksheet (WS 3.9)
- "Illustration Checklist" (WS 3.10)
- "Collaborate Create Competencies Rubric" (Appendix A.3)

Noticing Illustrations

Setting
» Light blue background
» Black tree trunks and branches
» Purple shapes for leaves and bushes

Characters
» Purple skin
» Black clothes
» No mouths
» White eyes with black pupils
» Tassels on three hats

Squirrel
» Pink and purple fur
» Orange eyes with black pupils

Text
» White words
» Only three words

What will you need to create the next page?
» Large piece of blue construction paper
» Scraps of blue, purple, black, white, orange, and pink construction paper
» Glue
» Scissors

Lesson Day 1

1. Ask learners if they would like to help author Chris Haughton add another page to his book. Explain that they will illustrate the characters catching the squirrel that's in the book. They will use the same color palette and characters.

2. Open the book to the final page. Ask the following questions and write responses on the "Noticing Illustrations" anchor chart (AC 3.6).
   – "What do you notice about this page?"
   – "How was the setting made?"
   – "How were the characters illustrated?"
   – "What do you notice about the text?"
   – "What will we need to illustrate the characters catching the squirrel?"

3. Explain that learners will develop a group plan to make their illustration.
4. Pass out the "Group Illustration" worksheet (WS 3.9).

Lesson Day 2

1. Tell learners that today they will illustrate their page of the characters catching the squirrel. They will use the "Group Illustration" worksheets (WS 3.9) from the previous lesson to guide their work.
2. Explain that learners will use a checklist to make sure their illustration matches the illustrations in *Shh! We Have a Plan.*
3. Pass out the "Illustration Checklist" (WS 3.10). Read the list together. Ask learners if anything needs to be added to the list.
4. Pass out the "Group Illustration" worksheet (WS 3.9) from the previous lesson.
5. Assess the "Group Illustration" worksheet (WS 3.9) using the "Collaborate Create Competencies Rubric" (Appendix A.3).

SHARE LESSON

Objective
Learners will present their illustrations and ask for feedback.

AASL Standards Framework for Learners: III.C.1. Learners work productively with others to solve problems by soliciting and responding to feedback from others.

Lesson Duration
45–50 minutes

Materials
- An illustration created by the educator for modeling purposes
- "Feedback" anchor chart (AC 3.7)
- Markers
- "Feedback for Projects" worksheet (Appendix B.10)
- "Feedback Reflection" worksheet (WS 3.11)
- "Collaborate Share Competencies Rubric" (Appendix A.3)

Feedback

What does feedback look like?
» Looking at the person while speaking to him or her
» Pointing to items of discussion
» Having a kind face

What does feedback sound like?
» "I like the way you . . ."
» "Can you tell me more about . . . ?"
» "Have you thought about . . . ?"
» "I wonder about . . ."

What do we do with feedback?
» Reflect
» Try new ideas

Why is feedback important?
» To make sure the message is clear
» To get different ideas
» To make a better product

Lesson

1. Introduce the lesson by asking learners to think of a time someone taught them how to do something. What words of advice did the person offer to help the learner get better?

2. Define the word *feedback*. Explain that you and the collaborating educator are going to model what giving feedback looks like and sounds like.

3. Show an illustration you made for the *Shh! We Have a Plan* project. The picture should include elements that work well with the book and elements that need improvements.

4. Tell the collaborating educator that you would really appreciate getting some feedback about the illustration.

5. Explain the illustration. Ask the following questions:
   - "Is my message clear?"
   - "Do you have suggestions to make it better?"
   - "What do you like about the illustration?"

6. Tell the collaborating educator ahead of time to begin feedback by giving compliments. Then offer feedback to improve the illustration.

7. Say, "Thank you for the feedback. You made some great points, and I'll consider them for my final illustration."

8. Ask the following questions and record responses on the "Feedback" anchor chart (AC 3.7).

   - "What does feedback look like?"
   - "What does feedback sound like?"
   - "What do we do with feedback?"
   - "Why is feedback important?"

9. Explain that groups will take turns presenting their illustrations. The audience will fill out the "Feedback for Projects" worksheet (Appendix B.10) after each presentation.
10. Collect the "Feedback for Projects" worksheets (Appendix B.10) and deliver them to the groups to read and discuss. Ask learners to reflect on feedback by filling out the "Feedback Reflection" worksheets (WS 3.11).
11. Assess responses with the "Collaborate Share Competencies Rubric" (Appendix A.3).

GROW LESSON

Objective
Learners will reflect on how well they listened to the ideas of others.

AASL Standards Framework for Learners: III.D.1. Learners actively participate with others in learning situations by actively contributing to group discussions.

Lesson Duration
45–50 minutes

Materials
- *Creatubbles,* an **AASL Best Website for Teaching and Learning**
- Computer lab or mobile devices
- "What Do Supportive Comments Look Like?" anchor chart (AC 3.8)
- Markers
- "Collaborate Grow Competencies Rubric" (Appendix A.3)

★ Creatubbles offers extensive support to use its website and app. Read the tips before getting started with learners. Create a project gallery for Shh! We Have a Plan and add a description.

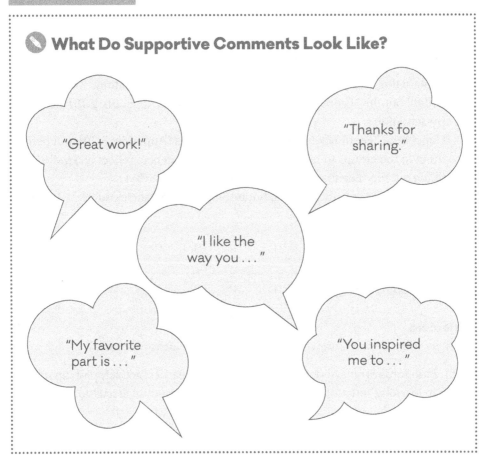

What Do Supportive Comments Look Like?

"Great work!"

"Thanks for sharing."

"I like the way you ... "

"My favorite part is ... "

"You inspired me to ... "

Lesson

1. Ask learners why it's important to be nice to people they meet. Enrich the conversation by asking if we should be nice to people on social media. What does it look like to give nice comments online? Write responses on the "What Do Supportive Comments Look Like?" anchor chart (AC 3.8).

2. Explain that learners are going to take pictures of their illustrations and upload them to a safe website/app for children. Everyone with access to the website/app will see their illustrations. People can "like" their work and share comments. Explain that all comments are reviewed before they are shared with the public. Tell learners about the translation feature that allows everyone from around the world to read comments in their own language.

3. Model how to upload work to the project gallery. Demonstrate the features on the website/app.

4. Allow learners to view other projects and make comments once they upload their project.
5. Assess work with the "Collaborate Grow Competencies Rubric" (Appendix A.3).

Post-Assessment

- Pass out the "Making a Plan" worksheet (WS 3.7).
- Read the directions with learners.
- Direct learners to circle the word "Post-Assessment" at the top of the page to distinguish this from the initial assessment.
- Assess responses with the "Collaborate Share Competencies Rubric" (Appendix A.3).
- Compare results with the pre-assessment.

WORKSHEET 3.7

MAKING A PLAN

Name: _____

Pre-Assessment/Post-Assessment

Directions: What does a group need to make a plan? Write a list of ideas.

- _____

- _____

- _____

- _____

- _____

- _____

- _____

- _____

- _____

- _____

- _____

- _____

- _____

- _____

- _____

SQUIRREL CATCHING PLAN

Names of Group Members:

- _____ • _____

- _____ • _____

- _____ • _____

Help the characters in *Shh! We Have a Plan* catch the squirrel at the end of the story. Follow the steps below to make a plan.

- ☐ Take turns sharing ideas.
- ☐ Listen to all ideas.
- ☐ Make suggestions or add to ideas.
- ☐ Agree on a plan.

Describe the plan to catch a squirrel.

_____

_____

_____

_____

_____

_____

_____

_____

_____

_____

WORKSHEET 3.9

GROUP ILLUSTRATION

Names of Group Members:

- _____ • _____

- _____ • _____

- _____ • _____

Directions: Follow the steps below to plan your illustration.

How will you illustrate the page? Discuss as a group and draw a sketch.
Add labels to your illustration.

What will we need? Discuss and write a list below:

- _____ • _____

- _____ • _____

- _____ • _____

What jobs will everyone have? Discuss and list below:

- _____ • _____

- _____ • _____

- _____ • _____

Our illustration has . . .

- ☐ a blue background.
- ☐ trees with black trunks and branches.
- ☐ purple leaves and bushes.

- ☐ a pink and purple squirrel that is being captured by four characters dressed in black.
- ☐ only a few words.

ILLUSTRATION CHECKLIST

Group Members:

- _____   - _____

- _____   - _____

- _____   - _____

Follow this checklist to make sure your illustration works with *Shh! We Have A Plan* by Chris Haughton.

Our illustration has . . .

- ☐ a blue background.
- ☐ trees with black trunks and branches.
- ☐ purple leaves and bushes.

- ☐ a pink and purple squirrel that is being captured by four characters dressed in black.
- ☐ only a few words.

ILLUSTRATION CHECKLIST

Group Members:

- _____   - _____

- _____   - _____

- _____   - _____

Follow this checklist to make sure your illustration works with *Shh! We Have A Plan* by Chris Haughton.

Our illustration has . . .

- ☐ a blue background.
- ☐ trees with black trunks and branches.
- ☐ purple leaves and bushes.

- ☐ a pink and purple squirrel that is being captured by four characters dressed in black.
- ☐ only a few words.

FEEDBACK REFLECTION

What did you notice about the feedback from your peers?

_____

_____

_____

_____

_____

Did you find the feedback helpful?

_____

_____

_____

_____

_____

How will it change your final presentation?

_____

_____

_____

_____

_____

HOW CAN WE WORK TOGETHER TO REPURPOSE MATERIALS?

Shared Foundation: Collaboration
Featured Book: *The Branch* by Mireille Messier

Summary

What would you do if your most prized possession broke? Would you find a way to repurpose it? In *The Branch,* by Mireille Messier, a little girl is distraught when her favorite tree branch breaks in an ice storm. The branch provided a place for her to imagine and dream. Can she use her imagination to make her broken treasure into something wonderful? This richly illustrated picture book tells the story of how a collaborative team reinvents a piece of wood. Learners will enjoy following the team effort in the story to repurpose recycled materials.

Pre-Assessment

- Pass out the "Reaching Goals Together" worksheet (WS 3.12).
- Ask learners to highlight or circle "Pre-Assessment" at the top of the worksheet.
- Assess responses with the "Collaborate Think Competencies Rubric" (Appendix A.3).

THINK LESSON

Objective

Learners will work together to design a useful product out of discarded materials.

AASL Standards Framework for Learners: III.A.2. Learners identify collaborative opportunities by developing new understandings through engagement in a learning group.

Lesson Duration

50–60 minutes

Materials

- Copy of *The Branch* by Mireille Messier
- *"The Branch"* anchor chart (AC 3.9)
- Paper
- Pencils
- Recycled materials randomly distributed on work tables
- "Seeing Potential" worksheet (WS 3.13)
- "Collaborate Think Competencies Rubric" (Appendix A.3)

The Branch

What was the problem in the story?

» The girl's favorite branch broke.

What did Mr. Frank and the girl need to solve the problem?

» An idea   » Tools   » Teamwork

» A plan   » Time

Lesson

1. Introduce the lesson by asking learners to think of a time when they worked with someone to fix something. What did they fix? How did they work as a team to fix the broken item?
2. Explain that the book you are about to read is about a young girl and her neighbor who work together to fix something.
3. Tell learners that as you read the story, their job is to look for evidence of people working together to solve a problem.
4. Ask the following questions as you read:
   - "What is the girl looking at? How does she feel? How do you know?" (cover)
   - "What is the illustrator telling us on this page?" (title page)
   - "What do you predict is making the loud noises?" (p. 4)
   - "How is the girl feeling on this page? How do you know?" (p. 9)
   - "What can you infer about Mr. Frank on this page?" (p. 16)
   - "Why are Mr. Frank's questions important?" (p. 18)
   - "What's important to remember on this page? Why do you think so?" (p. 19)
   - "What's important to remember on this page? Why do you think so?" (p. 21)
   - "Summarize what's happening on these pages." (pp. 24–27)
5. End the story by asking learners what they noticed about how Mr. Frank and the young girl worked together to solve a problem. Write the responses on the *"The Branch"* anchor chart (AC 3.9).
6. Explain that learners are going to collaborate with a group to find the potential in the recycled materials.
7. Read the directions on the "Seeing Potential" worksheet (WS 3.13). Form groups of learners and give each group a "Seeing Potential" worksheet (WS 3.13) to complete. Save responses to assess learning with the "Collaborate Think Competencies Rubric" (Appendix A.3).

📌 *Place recycled materials in a tub or box and label the container with the table number. This technique will make setup for the next lesson easy.*

CREATE LESSON

Objective
Learners will build their ideas.

AASL Standards Framework for Learners: III.B.2. Learners participate in personal, social, and intellectual networks by establishing connections with other learners to build on their own prior knowledge and create new knowledge.

Lesson Duration
50–60 minutes

Materials
- Completed "Seeing Potential" worksheets (WS 3.13) from the previous lesson
- Recycled materials (place the same materials on the same tables as for the previous lesson)
- Glue, tape
- Scissors
- Crayons, markers
- *Seesaw* app, an **AASL Best App for Teaching and Learning**
- Mobile devices
- Copy of *The Branch* by Mireille Messier
- "What Does COLLABORATION Look Like?" anchor chart (AC 3.10)
- "Collaborate Create Competencies Rubric" (Appendix A.3)

ANCHOR CHART 3.10

What Does COLLABORATION Look Like?

» People are working together.
» Everyone has a job.

» People are focused.
» People offer assistance.

★ *If you are unfamiliar with the Seesaw app, take some time to explore this valuable platform. Create a class and print a QR code for easy access. Give students time to play around with it before starting this lesson.*

Lesson

1. Inform learners that today they will collaborate with their group to make something from their recycled materials.

2. Open *The Branch* to page 24. Ask, "What does collaboration look like?" Show the next three pages. Record responses on the "What Does COLLABORATION Look Like?" anchor chart (AC 3.10).

3. Explain that one person in the group will use the *Seesaw* app to take pictures of learners collaborating on their project. The pictures should resemble the illustrations on pages 24–27 of *The Branch*. Learners can add a description with the photos or simply write #collaboration.

4. Send learners to their tables to begin creating something out of the recycled materials.

5. Assess the images on the *Seesaw* app with the "Collaborate Create Competencies Rubric" (Appendix A.3).

SHARE LESSON

Objective
Learners will invite others to view their product and ask for feedback.

AASL Standards Framework for Learners: III.C.1. Learners work productively with others to solve problems by soliciting and responding to feedback from others.

Lesson Duration
45–50 minutes

Materials
- "Feedback" anchor chart (AC 3.7)
- Markers
- Finished projects
- *DIY,* an **AASL Best Website for Teaching and Learning**
- Projector

- "Feedback for Projects" worksheet (Appendix B.10)
- Pencils
- "Collaborate Share Competencies Rubric" (Appendix A.3)

Lesson

- Tell learners that they will share their work online to inspire others from around the globe.
- Explain that before they share their work online, they should ask for feedback from their classmates about their project. Ask, "Why is feedback important?"
- Visit a project on the *DIY* website. Model what feedback looks like by saying a few nice things about the project and then offering suggestions.
- Ask learners what they noticed about your feedback. Write responses on the "Feedback" anchor chart (AC 3.7).
- Invite groups to present and explain their projects.
- Ask the audience to give feedback on the presentations by filling out the "Feedback for Projects" worksheet (Appendix B.10).
- Assess learning with the "Collaborate Share Competencies Rubric" (Appendix A.3).

GROW LESSON

Objective

Learners will upload pictures of their projects on the *DIY* website and comment on other projects.

AASL Standards Framework for Learners: III.D.1. Learners actively participate with others in learning situations by actively contributing to group discussions.

Lesson Duration

45–50 minutes

Materials

- *DIY*, also available online and as an app, is recognized as an **AASL Best Website for Teaching and Learning**
- Mobile devices
- Projects from the previous lesson
- "What Do Supportive Comments Look Like?" anchor chart (AC 3.8)
- "Collaborate Grow Competencies Rubric" (Appendix A.3)

★ *Familiarize yourself with the DIY app and website before using it with learners. Register your class so learners can upload their pictures and make comments.*

Lesson

1. Inform learners that they will upload a picture of their project on an online social platform called *DIY*. Tell them that the site is safe for children. Explain that once their image is uploaded to the website, learners from around the world can comment on their project. Learners can also comment on other projects.

2. Ask, "What do supportive comments look like? Let's see if we can find some on the *DIY* website." Choose a project and read the comments together. Ask what learners think about the comments. Are the comments helpful? Are they nice? Write some examples of supportive comments on the "What Do Supportive Comments Look Like?" anchor chart (AC 3.8).

3. Model how to take a picture and upload it to *DIY*. Demonstrate how to write comments.

4. Pass out mobile devices with the downloaded *DIY* app.

5. Assess learning with the "Collaborate Grow Competencies Rubric" (Appendix A.3).

Post-Assessment

- Pass out the "Reaching Goals Together" worksheet (WS 3.12).
- Ask learners to highlight or circle "Post-Assessment" at the top of the worksheet.
- Assess responses with the "Collaborate Think Competencies Rubric" (Appendix A.3).
- Compare responses with the pre-assessment.

WORKSHEET 3.12

REACHING GOALS TOGETHER

Name: _____

Pre-Assessment/Post-Assessment

How can we work together to meet a common goal?

_____

_____

_____

_____

_____

_____

_____

_____

_____

_____

_____

_____

_____

_____

SEEING POTENTIAL

Names of Group Members:

- _____ • _____

- _____ • _____

- _____ • _____

Follow the steps below:

1) What can the recycled materials on your table become? List the group's ideas. Make sure all members contribute.

- _____

- _____

- _____

- _____

- _____

- _____

2) Choose one idea to make with the recycled materials. How did you decide what to make?

_____

_____

_____

_____

_____

_____

_____

Curate Lessons

KEY COMMITMENT
Make meaning for oneself and others by collecting, organizing, and sharing resources of personal relevance.

HOW CAN WE COLLECT IMPORTANT INFORMATION TO SHARE WITH OTHERS?

Shared Foundation: Curate
Featured Book: *Antsy Ansel: Ansel Adams, a Life in Nature* by Cindy Jenson-Elliott

Summary

Think of a time when you saw something that took your breath away. What was it? How did you share your experience? Ansel Adams was a passionate outdoorsman. He had a talent for capturing amazing landscapes with his camera. This is the story of what compelled Adams to take environmental photographs. Learners will appreciate reading how he left traditional schooling to find lessons in nature. While reading this engaging biography, students will understand why Adams took pictures of the national parks. His photographs will inspire learners to curate resources about the national parks for future reference.

Pre-Assessment

- Pass out the "Collecting Important Information" worksheet (WS 4.1).
- Ask learners to think about why they search for information. How do they collect the information they find? Write their answers on the lines provided.
- Ask learners to highlight or circle "Pre-Assessment" at the top of the worksheet.
- Assess responses with the "Curate Think Competencies Rubric" (Appendix A.4).
- Save worksheets to establish a baseline for competencies.

THINK LESSON

Objective
Learners will ask questions about the national parks.

AASL Standards Framework for Learners: IV.A.1. Learners act on an information need by determining the need to gather information.

Lesson Duration
2 lessons, 50–60 minutes each

Materials
- "Why Do We Gather Information?" anchor chart (AC 4.1)
- Markers
- Copy of *Antsy Ansel: Ansel Adams, a Life in Nature* by Cindy Jenson-Elliott
- "National Parks Observations" worksheet (WS 4.2)
- Access to the website *The Hidden Worlds of the National Parks* (see the "Online Resources" section at the end of the book for the web address)
- Computer lab or mobile devices
- Pencils
- "Curate Think Competencies Rubric" (Appendix A.4)

> ★ *If you have Google Cardboard Headsets, try using the Google Expeditions app, an AASL Best App for Teaching and Learning, for a virtual tour of the national parks.*

Lesson Day 1
1. Gather learners to read *Antsy Ansel: Ansel Adams, A Life in Nature* by Cindy Jenson-Elliott.
2. As you look at the cover, ask the following questions:
    - "Read the title and look at the picture. What can we expect to learn from this book?"
    - "Look closely at the illustration. What questions do you have?"
    - "When does this story takes place? How can you tell?"

3. Explain that while you read the story, learners should recognize how Ansel Adams collected information about nature.

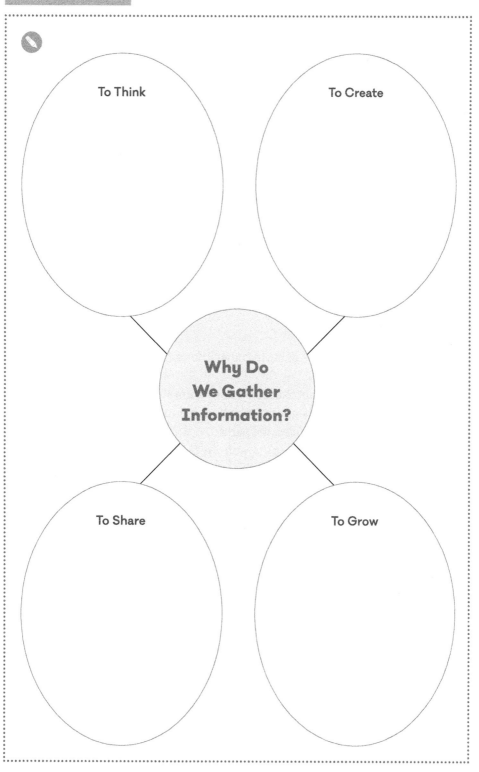

To Think

To Create

**Why Do
We Gather
Information?**

To Share

To Grow

4. As you read, ask learners the following questions:
   - "What did we learn about Ansel Adams so far?" (p. 9)
   - "How does Ansel Adams remember his outdoor explorations?" (p. 11)
   - "If you were with Ansel Adams at the fair, what would you do to remember the day?" (p. 13)
   - "How can the people in the open-air bus remember what they saw at Valley View?" (p. 14)
   - "How does Ansel Adams record what he sees in nature?" (p. 17)
   - "What was important to Ansel Adams? How can you tell?" (pp. 22–23)
   - "What does the author want us to know on this page?" (p. 24)

5. End the story by pointing to the main idea bubble on the "Why Do We Gather Information?" anchor chart (AC 4.1). Explain that taking pictures is another way to collect information.

6. Ask, "Why did Ansel Adams take pictures? To think? To create? To share? To grow? Why do you think so?" Write responses on the "Why Do We Gather Information?" anchor chart (AC 4.1).

Lesson Day 2

1. Tell learners that they are going to gather information about national parks over the next few days.

2. Ask, "Why would we want to collect information about national parks?" Explain that today learners will begin making observations and taking notes while going on a virtual tour of some national parks.

3. Show learners how to access the website *The Hidden Worlds of the National Parks*.

4. Pass out the "National Parks Observations" worksheet (WS 4.2) and pencils. Tell learners to draw what they notice and describe what they see.

5. End the lesson by asking learners to think about why they collected information about national parks. Direct students to write their answer in the space provided at the bottom of the "National Parks Observations" worksheet (WS 4.2).

6. Collect the worksheets and review the final answer to assess Competencies using the "Curate Think Competencies Rubric" (Appendix A.4).

CREATE LESSON

Objective
Learners will search different databases and websites that will help them learn about the national parks.

AASL Standards Framework for Learners: IV.B.1. Learners gather information appropriate to the task by seeking a variety of sources.

Lesson Duration
45–50 minutes

Materials
- "Multiple Sources" anchor chart (AC 4.2)
- "Helpful Websites" worksheet (WS 4.3)
- Computer lab or mobile devices
- Access to databases and child-friendly websites curated on the library website
- "Curate Create Competencies Rubric" (Appendix A.4)

ANCHOR CHART 4.2

 Multiple Sources

Why should we look at more than one website when we collect information?
» Some websites could have the wrong information.
» Some websites have updated information.
» Some websites are easier to read and navigate.

What keywords should we search?
» "national parks"
» Names of national parks

Lesson
1. Introduce the lesson by telling students they will visit different databases and websites to find the most helpful resources about the national parks.
2. Ask, "Why is it important to look at more than one website when we are gathering information?" Write responses on the "Multiple Sources" anchor chart (AC 4.2).
3. Direct learners to your library website where they can access links to databases and kid-friendly search engines.
4. Model how to open a website.
5. Ask the following questions:
   – "What should I type in the search bar to find information about the national parks?"
   – "Why is it important to search the Internet using keywords rather than typing a complete sentence?"

6. Write keyword suggestions on the "Multiple Sources" anchor chart (AC 4.2).
7. Type the keywords in the search bar and review the results together.
8. Model how to read the descriptions of the websites to decide if the website should be opened.
9. Ask, "Will this website help me learn about the national parks?"
10. Tell learners that when they find a helpful website about the national parks, they will write the title of the website, the web address, and the date that they opened the website. Model how to locate and record information on the "Helpful Websites" worksheet (WS 4.3).
11. Collect worksheets when learners finish working. Use the "Curate Create Competencies Rubric" to assess worksheets (Appendix A.4).

SHARE LESSON

Objective
Learners will curate helpful websites for research on the national parks.

AASL Standards Framework for Learners: IV.C.2. Learners exchange information resources within and beyond their learning community by contributing to collaboratively constructed information sites by ethically using and reproducing others' work.

Lesson Duration
45–50 minutes

Materials
- "Posting on the Internet: What Should We Consider Before Posting?" anchor chart (AC 4.3)
- Link to a shared collaborative web page like *Padlet,* an **AASL Best Website for Teaching and Learning**.
- Access to the library website
- Projector
- "Helpful Websites" worksheet (WS 4.3) from the previous lesson
- "Curate Share Competencies Rubric" (Appendix A.4)
- Pencils

ANCHOR CHART 4.3

 **Posting on the Internet:
What Should We Consider Before Posting?**

» Why are we posting?   » Is it true?

» Is it kind?   » Are words spelled correctly?

» Is it helpful?

Prepare for the Lesson

1. Create a collaborative web page using a platform like *Padlet*.
2. Allow public comments to the web page to make it easy for learners to participate.
3. Set up the web page with the title "Helpful Websites about the National Parks."
4. Copy the link to the collaborative web page and paste it on your library website.

Lesson

1. Invite learners to share what they liked about the national parks websites. Ask, "If we were to put all of our favorite websites together, do you think people would appreciate the curated list of websites? Why do you think so? Who do you think would be interested in looking at the websites?"
2. Inform learners that you set up a collaborative web page so that anyone with Internet access can find their site and add to it. Knowing that anyone can read what they wrote, what should they consider before posting? Add ideas to the "Posting on the Internet: What Should We Consider Before Posting?" anchor chart (AC 4.3).
3. Demonstrate how to open the shared collaborative web page.
4. Model how to type the title of a website, create a hyperlink, and include a description. Tell learners to be proud of what they write and add their initials next to their post.
5. Explain that they will see many classmates working on the collaborative web page. Learners will have fun seeing everyone work together.
6. Review the collaborative web page to assess Competencies using the "Curate Share Competencies Rubric" (Appendix A.4).

GROW LESSON

Objective
Learners will visit websites about the national parks to find out whether the content is useful.

AASL Standards Framework for Learners: IV.D.1. Learners select and organize information for a variety of audiences by performing ongoing analysis of and reflection on the quality, usefulness, and accuracy of curated resources.

Lesson Duration
40–50 minutes

Materials
- "Useful Website Checklist" worksheet (WS 4.4)
- "How Can I Tell If a Website Is Useful?" anchor chart (AC 4.4)
- Computer lab or mobile devices
- Access to the "Helpful Websites about the National Parks" collaborative web page from previous lesson
- "Curate Grow Competencies Rubric" (Appendix A.4)

ANCHOR CHART 4.4

 How Can I Tell If a Website Is Useful?

» Is it easy to read?
» Does the information answer my questions?
» Does it have recent information?
» Can I contact the owner of the website?
» Can I read about the owner of the website?

Lesson
1. Introduce the lesson by asking the following questions:
   - "Who can add websites to our collaborative web page?"
   - "Should we monitor the web page to make sure people are posting helpful comments and websites?"
   - "How can we decide if the websites will help others learn about the national parks?"

2. Say, "Let's develop a checklist to help us decide if websites are helpful. What should we consider?" Add responses to the "How Can I Tell If a Website Is Useful?" anchor chart (AC 4.4).

3. Open the "Helpful Websites about the National Parks" collaborative web page. Click on one of the sites a student posted and run through the checklist with students.

4. Show learners how to find the author by looking at the "About" tab and the "Contact Us" tab. If none exists, scroll down to the bottom of the page to locate the information. Let students know that if they can't find the author or contact information, they should consider finding another website.

5. Ask, "Why is it important to find out when the information was written?" Facilitate a discussion about why up-to-date information is the most accurate.

6. Show learners how to find the copyright date of a website by scrolling to the bottom of the page. Point out the dates of articles posted on the site.

7. Ask, "Why is it important to think about why an author would write information on a website?"

8. Direct learners to create a checklist of their own to determine if the websites are helpful. They can use any of the requirements shared in the lesson. They will write their checklist on the "Useful Website Checklist" worksheet (WS 4.4).

9. Collect finished work to assess competencies using the "Curate Grow Competencies Rubric" (Appendix A.4).

Post-Assessment

- Tell learners you would like to see how much they learned over the past few days about collecting information. Explain that they are to answer the two questions on the "Collecting Important Information" worksheet (WS 4.1).
- Pass out the "Collecting Important Information" worksheet (WS 4.1).
- Ask learners to circle the word "Post-Assessment" at the top of the page to distinguish this from the initial assessment.
- Assess responses with the "Curate Think Competencies Rubric" (Appendix A.4).
- Compare responses with the pre-assessment.

COLLECTING IMPORTANT INFORMATION

Name: _____

Pre-Assessment/Post-Assessment

Directions: Answer the questions below.

Why do people search for information?

_____

_____

_____

_____

_____

_____

How can we collect the information we find?

_____

_____

_____

_____

_____

_____

NATIONAL PARKS OBSERVATIONS

Name: _____

Directions: Take a virtual trip to a national park. What do you notice? What do you see? Collect information about the national parks by illustrating what you see in the box below.

What did you learn about the national park you visited?

_____

_____

_____

Why did you collect information about the national parks today?

_____

_____

_____

HELPFUL WEBSITES

Name: _____

Directions: Search for websites that will help you find answers to your questions about the national parks. Write the title, the address, and the day you opened the website below.

Title: _____

Address: _____

Date Opened: _____

Title: _____

Address: _____

Date Opened: _____

Title: _____

Address: _____

Date Opened: _____

Title: _____

Address: _____

Date Opened: _____

Title: _____

Address: _____

Date Opened: _____

USEFUL WEBSITE CHECKLIST

Name: _____

Directions: What should we look for on a website to determine if the information is accurate? Create a "Useful Website Checklist" with important things to look at when determining if a website is helpful. Use your checklist to evaluate a website.

Website Title: _____

Website Address: _____

1) _____ **YES** **NO**

2) _____ **YES** **NO**

3) _____ **YES** **NO**

4) _____ **YES** **NO**

5) _____ **YES** **NO**

6) _____ **YES** **NO**

7) _____ **YES** **NO**

8) _____ **YES** **NO**

9) _____ **YES** **NO**

WHY IS IT IMPORTANT TO KEEP TRACK OF WHAT WE READ AND WHAT WE WANT TO READ?

Shared Foundation: Curate
Featured Book: *Wanted! Ralfy Rabbit, Book Burglar* by Emily MacKenzie

Summary

Ralfy Rabbit is a passionate reader. He finds books irresistible. He creates booklists and recommends titles to friends and family. Unfortunately, his love for books is so over-the-top that he begins to steal them, until he learns about a place called the library. After reading this delightful story about a rabbit who loves to read, children will want to curate a booklist of their own.

Pre-Assessment

- Ask learners to complete the "Keeping Track of Books" worksheet (WS 4.5).
- Ask learners to highlight or circle "Pre-Assessment" at the top of the worksheet.
- Assess responses with the "Curate Create Competencies Rubric" (Appendix A.4).

THINK LESSON

Objective

Learners will curate a list of books.

AASL Standards Framework for Learners: IV.A.1. Learners act on an information need by determining the need to gather information.

Lesson Duration

45–50 minutes

Materials

- A copy of *Wanted! Ralfy Rabbit, Book Burglar* by Emily MacKenzie
- "Examples of Keeping Track of Books" anchor chart (AC 4.5)
- Pencils
- Markers
- "My Booklist" worksheet (WS 4.6)
- "Curate Think Competencies Rubric" (Appendix A.4)

Examples of Keeping Track of Books

Ralfy Rabbit	Arthur
» List of books that Ralfy has read, with a rating system » List of favorite books » List of books that he wants to read » Recommendations for friends and family	» Arthur organizes his books by topic.

Lesson

1. Show learners the copy of *Wanted! Ralfy Rabbit, Book Burglar* by Emily MacKenzie.
2. Say, "Read the title and look at the illustration on the cover of this book. Make a prediction about the story."
3. Explain that as you read the book, the learners' job is to notice how Ralfy Rabbit and a boy named Arthur keep track of the books they read. Write responses on the "Examples of Keeping Track of Books" anchor chart (AC 4.5).
4. Review pages 3–4 with learners. Explain that they will pick one of Ralfy's lists and create their own list of books.
5. Pass out the "My Booklist" worksheet (WS 4.6).
6. Save responses to assess progress with the "Curate Think Competencies Rubric" (Appendix A.4).

 ## CREATE LESSON

Objective
Learners will develop a system to rate books and organize titles on virtual shelves.

AASL Standards Framework for Learners: IV.B.4. Learners gather information appropriate to the task by organizing information by priority, topic, or other systematic scheme.

Lesson Duration
45–50 minutes

Materials

- *Bookopolis,* an **AASL Best Website for Teaching and Learning**
- Projector
- Access to the Internet
- Computer lab or mobile devices
- "Rating Books" anchor chart (AC 4.6)
- Markers
- Slips of paper with usernames and passwords to sign into *Bookopolis*
- "Book Rating" worksheet (WS 4.7)
- "Curate Create Competencies Rubric" (Appendix A.4)

ANCHOR CHART 4.6

 Rating Books

What qualities should a book have in order to earn a 5-star rating?

- » Great writing
- » Clear message
- » Engaging illustrations
- » Enjoyable to read

What qualities should a book have in order to earn a 3-star rating?

- » Book is somewhat interesting
- » Illustrations are forgettable

What qualities should a book have in order to earn a 1-star rating?

- » Poor writing
- » No story line
- » Dull illustrations

 *Familiarize yourself with **Bookopolis** before the lesson.*

Set up a class by assigning a username and a password for each learner.

Lesson

1. Invite learners to share their favorite part of *Wanted! Ralfy Rabbit, Book Burglar*.
2. Ask learners to rate the book by giving it 1 to 5 stars, with 5 being the best. How did learners decide how to rate the book? Write responses on the "Rating Books" anchor chart (AC 4.6).
3. Explain that they will visit an online site that allows learners to organize and rate book titles. Point out that the website is a safe place for young learners. Model how to log on to the site. Search for *Wanted! Ralfy Rabbit, Book Burglar*. Demonstrate how to rate the book.
4. Distribute usernames and passwords to access *Bookopolis*.
5. Ask learners to fill out the "Book Rating" worksheet (WS 4.7) after they rate the book online.
6. Collect the "Book Rating" worksheets (WS 4.7) to assess learning with the "Curate Create Competencies Rubric" (Appendix A.4).

SHARE LESSON

Objective

Learners will write a book review and read reviews by other contributors.

AASL Standards Framework for Learners: IV.C.3. Learners exchange information resources within and beyond their learning community by joining with others to compare and contrast information derived from collaboratively constructed information sites.

Lesson Duration

45–50 minutes

Materials

- *Bookopolis,* an **AASL Best Website for Teaching and Learning**
- "Book Reviews" anchor chart (AC 4.7)
- Slips of paper with usernames and passwords for *Bookopolis*
- Markers
- Computer lab or mobile devices
- "Curate Share Competencies Rubric" (Appendix A.4)

ANCHOR CHART 4.7

 Book Reviews

How to Write a Book Review

» Start by engaging the reader with a question or an interesting statement.

- "If you want to learn about snakes, you must read this book!"
- "How do you feel about snakes? If you love them as much as I do, you'll want to read this book!"
- "Did you know that snakes are quite amazing? Read this book to find out why."

» Write two to three sentences that support the first statement about the book.

- "This easy-to-read book is full of captions and labels. The pictures are amazing!"

» Conclude the review with one sentence that summarizes the main point.

- "You'll think differently about snakes after reading this informative book."

Lesson

1. Introduce the lesson by asking learners why book reviews are important. Explain that they are going to write a book review for *Wanted! Ralfy Rabbit, Book Burglar.*
2. Say, "Let's look at some of the book reviews on *Bookopolis* and find reviews that are helpful." Find an example. Ask learners what makes it a helpful review.
3. Discuss the components of a book review and write them on the "Book Reviews" anchor chart (AC 4.7).
4. Tell children to search for *Wanted! Ralfy Rabbit, Book Burglar* on *Bookopolis* and add the book to their shelf. Instruct them to write a review.
5. Read other reviews and click the "thumbs-up" sign to "like" the review.
6. Assess reviews with the "Curate Share Competencies Rubric" (Appendix A.4).

 ## GROW LESSON

Objective

Learners will visit classmates' shelves and comment on their recommendations.

AASL Standards Framework for Learners: IV.D.3. Learners select and organize information for a variety of audiences by openly communicating curation processes for others to use, interpret, and validate.

Lesson Duration
45–50 minutes

Materials
- "Posting Comments" anchor chart (AC 4.8)
- Marker
- *Bookopolis,* an **AASL Best Website for Teaching and Learning**
- Slips of paper with usernames and passwords for *Bookopolis*
- Computer lab or mobile devices
- "Curate Grow Competencies Rubric" (Appendix A.4)

ANCHOR CHART 4.8

Lesson
1. Ask learners what they like about using *Bookopolis.* Explain that today they will look at their classmates' shelves and write comments about the books they curated.
2. Ask, "Knowing that the whole world can read our comments, what should we consider before posting?"

3. Develop sentence starters for writing kind comments on the "Posting Comments" anchor chart (AC 4.8).
4. Distribute usernames and passwords.
5. Read comments to assess learning with the "Curate Grow Competencies Rubric" (Appendix A.4).

Post-Assessment

- Ask learners to complete the "Keeping Track of Books" worksheet (WS 4.5).
- Direct learners to circle the word "Post-Assessment" at the top of the page to distinguish this from the initial assessment.
- Assess responses with the "Curate Create Competencies Rubric" (Appendix A.4).
- Compare results with the pre-assessment to measure growth.

KEEPING TRACK OF BOOKS

Name: _____

Pre-Assessment/Post-Assessment

Directions: Describe how you keep track of the books you read.

_____

_____

_____

_____

_____

_____

_____

_____

_____

_____

_____

_____

_____

_____

_____

_____

_____

_____

_____

WORKSHEET 4.6

MY BOOKLIST

Name:

Title of List:

Directions:
- Write a list of books. It can be a list of your favorite books, books you are currently reading, books you want to read, or book recommendations.
- Decorate your booklist. See Ralfy Rabbit's lists for ideas.

BOOK RATING

Name: _____

Title of Book: *Wanted! Ralfy Rabbit, Book Burglar* by Emily MacKenzie

Book Rating:

How did you decide on the rating?

_____

_____

_____

_____

_____

_____

_____

_____

_____

_____

_____

_____

_____

WHY IS IT IMPORTANT TO USE MULTIPLE SOURCES TO LEARN ABOUT A TOPIC?

Shared Foundation: Curate
Featured Book: *Thirsty, Thirsty Elephants*
by Sandra Markle

Summary

Are you familiar with the saying "an elephant never forgets"? Well, it's true! There are some things they don't forget. In *Thirsty, Thirsty Elephants* by Sandra Markle, we learn that elephants can remember important things. When the elephants in the story face a drought, Grandmother Elephant remembers a watering hole from her youth. She leads the herd to the lake and saves them from dehydration. This story will intrigue readers and encourage them to learn more about the majestic elephant. Online tools will help learners curate resources to share with others.

Pre-Assessment
- Pass out the "Helpful Information" worksheet (WS 4.8).
- Direct learners to circle "Pre-Assessment" at the top of the worksheet.
- Assess skills with the "Curate Think Competencies Rubric" (Appendix A.4).

THINK LESSON

Objective
Learners will locate helpful resources to answer questions about elephants.

AASL Standards Framework for Learners: IV.A.1. Learners act on an information need by determining the need to gather information.

Lesson Duration
2 lessons, 45–50 minutes each

Materials
- Copy of *Thirsty, Thirsty Elephants* by Sandra Markle
- A younger classroom audience, with each young learner paired with an older learner

- "Questions We Have" anchor chart (AC 4.9)
- *Wonderopolis,* an **AASL Best Website for Teaching and Learning**
- Books about elephants
- Library databases
- Encyclopedias
- "Elephant Resources" worksheet (WS 4.9)
- "Curate Think Competencies Rubric" (Appendix A.4)

ANCHOR CHART 4.9

 Questions We Have

» Where is Tanzania?

» How long can an elephant live without water?

» How much water does an elephant need every day?

» How good is an elephant's memory?

» What can elephants do with their trunks?

Lesson Day 1

1. Tell learners they are going to help younger students find answers to their questions about elephants. Learners will curate resources that the younger audience can understand.

2. Invite the younger class in to read *Thirsty, Thirsty Elephants* by Sandra Markle.

3. Ask the following questions as you read the book, and write responses on the "Questions We Have" anchor chart (AC 4.9).
    - "What questions do you have about the setting?" (p. 1)
    - "What questions do you have after reading these pages?" (pp. 7–8)
    - "What are you wondering about after reading this page?" (p. 11)
    - "What can you infer about Grandmother Elephant's role?" (pp. 13–14)
    - "What can you infer about elephants so far?" (pp. 15–16)
    - "What questions do you have about these pages?" (pp. 19–20)

4. Tell the younger learners that the older learners are going to find resources to help them answer questions they have about elephants. Ask, "Is there anything else you wonder about elephants?" Write questions on the "Questions We Have" anchor chart (AC 4.9).

Lesson Day 2

1. Say, "What kind of information should we look for to answer questions about elephants? What should we think about when we are looking for resources for the early readers?"

2. Explain that some websites have a read-aloud feature to assist emerging readers. Model how to search for elephant information and use the read-aloud feature on *Wonderopolis.*
3. Model how to access the library databases.
4. Point to the collection of elephant books and encyclopedias. Invite learners to look through the materials to find appropriate books for emerging readers.
5. Learners will write the titles of websites and books on the "Elephant Resources" worksheet (WS 4.9).
6. Collect worksheets to assess learning using the "Curate Think Competencies Rubric" (Appendix A.4).

CREATE LESSON

Objective
Learners will refer to a checklist to determine whether a source is reliable.

AASL Standards Framework for Learners: IV.B.3. Learners gather information appropriate to the task by systematically questioning and assessing the validity and accuracy of information.

Lesson Duration
45–50 minutes

Materials
- *The Family Structure of Elephants* by Caitlin O'Connell-Rodwell, a TED-Ed video.
- "How Do I Know If the Information Is Reliable?" anchor chart (AC 4.10)
- Projector
- Computer
- "Resource Checklist" (WS 4.10)
- "Curate Create Competencies Rubric" (Appendix A.4)

Lesson
1. Introduce the lesson by asking learners about the elephant resources they discovered. What was their favorite resource?
2. Explain that learners need to take their resource search a step further. They need to make sure their resources are reliable. Why is that important?

"How Do I Know If the Information Is Reliable?"

Author:
- » Is the author an expert?
- » Is the author trying to persuade me to think or feel something?
- » What is the author's purpose?

Year of Publication:
- » How long ago was the information published?
- » Is there more recent information?

Verify Information with Other Sources:
- » Do other resources say the same thing?

3. Explain that one way to determine if information is reliable is to read about the author. Is the author an expert? Is the author trying to make you feel or think a certain way? What is the author's purpose? Write these ideas on the "How Do I Know If the Information Is Reliable?" anchor chart (AC 4.10).

4. Define the term *publication date*. Ask why the date matters. Write responses on the "How Do I Know If the Information Is Reliable?" anchor chart (AC 4.10).

5. Say, "We are going to look at a video clip about elephants and decide if the information is reliable." Visit the TED-Ed video *The Family Structure of Elephants* by Caitlin O'Connell-Rodwell. Read the description of the presenter. Ask, "Is she an elephant expert? What makes you think so?"

6. Discover the publication date presented at the beginning of the video. Ask, "How old is the information? Is it still reliable?" Ask, "Why is it important to look for recent information?"

7. Watch the video. Did some of the material verify the information in *Thirsty, Thirsty Elephants*? Why should that matter? Write responses on the "How Do I Know If the Information Is Reliable?" anchor chart (AC 4.10).

8. Explain that the same rules apply to books. Model how to find information about the author and the publication date in a book.

9. Tell learners that they are going to decide if the information they found about elephants is reliable. They will use a "Resource Checklist" (WS 4.10) to help them decide.

10. Check for understanding with the "Curate Create Competencies Rubric" (Appendix A.4).

SHARE LESSON

Objective
Learners will post the most reliable resources for elephant research on a social platform.

AASL Standards Framework for Learners: IV.C.3. Learners exchange information resources within and beyond their learning community by joining with others to compare and contrast information derived from collaboratively constructed information sites.

Lesson Duration
60 minutes

Materials
- *Padlet,* an **AASL Best Website for Teaching and Learning**
- "Resource Collection" anchor chart (AC 4.11)
- "Resource Description Checklist" (WS 4.11)
- Pencils
- "Curate Share Competencies Rubric" (Appendix A.4)

 Set up the **Padlet** board ahead of time. Share the link on your library website.

ANCHOR CHART 4.11

 Resource Collection

How Can We Share Reliable Resources with Others?
  » Create a display.
  » Make a flyer.
  » Present the resources.
  » List and describe the resources on a digital platform.

What Should We Include?
  » The title
  » The author
  » The publication date
  » A short description
  » Initials of the person posting

Lesson

1. Ask learners how many reliable resources they found about elephants. Say, "You worked hard finding resources for younger readers. You found reliable materials they could understand. We need to put all of your resources in one place so everyone can access the titles. Do you have any ideas about how to do this?" Write ideas on the "Resource Collection" anchor chart (AC 4.11).

2. Describe *Padlet*. Explain that it is a safe place to share and describe information. Model how to post comments. Tell learners that they will post their favorite elephant resource on *Padlet*. Discuss the elements to include in a post. Learners should include the resource title, the name of the author, the publication date, and a brief description. Show them how to add a weblink to the post. Write elements on the "Resource Collection" anchor chart (AC 4.11).

3. Point out that learners will see their friends posting at the same time. Expect to see repeated resources. Learners can compare and contrast different comments about duplicated titles.

4. Pass out the "Resource Description Checklist" worksheet (WS 4.11).

5. Check posts on *Padlet* to assess learning with the "Curate Share Competencies Rubric" (Appendix A.4).

GROW LESSON

Objective

Learners will present curated information to another class.

AASL Standards Framework for Learners: IV.D.3. Learners select and organize information for a variety of audiences by openly communicating curation processes for others to use, interpret, and validate.

Lesson Duration

2 lessons, 45–50 minutes each

Materials

- "Presenting Curated Resources" anchor chart (AC 4.12)
- Paper
- Crayons
- Markers
- Scissors
- Collection of elephant books
- Laptops or mobile devices
- "Curation Exit Slip" (WS 4.12)
- "Curate Grow Competencies Rubric" (Appendix A.4)

Presenting Curated Resources

» Gather books and display them.
» Create a flyer listing resources by material type.
» Display *Padlet*.

Lesson Day 1

1. Introduce the lesson by asking learners if they are ready to share their curated resources with another class.
2. Ask for ideas about how to make it easy for another class to find the learners' list of curated resources. Write ideas on the "Presenting Curated Resources" anchor chart (AC 4.12).
3. Form three groups of learners. Group 1 will collect the books and make a display. Group 2 will create a flyer that describes the elephant resource Padlet and includes the web address. Group 3 will practice presenting how to access and navigate the Padlet. Learners will choose the group they want to join.

 Work with the collaborating educator ahead of time to partner older learners with younger learners for this lesson.

Lesson Day 2

1. Invite a class to view the presentation. Each group will briefly describe their resources. Partner students with younger learners to assist them in accessing and reading information.
2. Ask younger learners to fill out the "Curation Exit Slip" worksheet (WS 4.12) after the session.
3. Assess the "Curation Exit Slip" worksheets (WS 4.12) with the "Curate Grow Competencies Rubric" (Appendix A.4).

Post-Assessment

- Pass out the "Helpful Information" worksheet (WS 4.8).
- Direct learners to circle the word "Post-Assessment" at the top of the page to distinguish this from the initial assessment.
- Assess skills with the "Curate Think Competencies Rubric" (Appendix A.4).
- Compare results with the pre-assessment to determine growth.

HELPFUL INFORMATION

Name: _____

Pre-Assessment/Post-Assessment

How can you tell if information is helpful?

_____

_____

_____

_____

_____

_____

_____

_____

_____

_____

_____

_____

_____

_____

ELEPHANT RESOURCES

Name: _____

1) What is the purpose for collecting information about elephants?

_____

_____

_____

_____

_____

2) List website titles here:

- _____

- _____

- _____

- _____

- _____

3) List book titles here:

- _____

- _____

- _____

- _____

- _____

WORKSHEET 4.10

RESOURCE CHECKLIST

Title of Publication: _____

Author: _____

Is the author's name listed?	**YES**	**NO**
Is the author an expert?	**YES**	**NO**
Is the author trying to persuade me to think or feel something?	**YES**	**NO**

What is the author's purpose?

_____

_____

_____

Year of Publication

What is the publication date? _____

How long ago was the information published? _____

Is there more recent information?   **YES**   **NO**

Verify Information with Other Sources

Do other resources say the same thing?   **YES**   **NO**

RESOURCE DESCRIPTION CHECKLIST

Name: _____

Directions: Follow the checklist below when posting your resource online.

Your post must have:

- ❏ The title of the resource
- ❏ The name of the author
- ❏ The year of publication
- ❏ A brief description (one to two sentences)

_____

_____

- ❏ Your initials _____

- -

RESOURCE DESCRIPTION CHECKLIST

Name: _____

Directions: Follow the checklist below when posting your resource online.

Your post must have:

- ❏ The title of the resource
- ❏ The name of the author
- ❏ The year of publication
- ❏ A brief description (one to two sentences)

_____

_____

- ❏ Your initials _____

WORKSHEET 4.12

CURATION EXIT SLIP

My Name:

My Partner's Name:

Did your partner show you where to find helpful information about elephants?

YES   NO

What was most helpful? Circle any of the choices below.

Display of Books   Resources on Flyer   Resources on *Padlet*

- -

CURATION EXIT SLIP

My Name:

My Partner's Name:

Did your partner show you where to find helpful information about elephants?

YES   NO

What was most helpful? Circle any of the choices below.

Display of Books   Resources on Flyer   Resources on *Padlet*

CHAPTER 5

Explore Lessons

KEY COMMITMENT
Discover and innovate in a growth mindset developed through experience and reflection.

HOW DO PEOPLE AND GROUPS DECIDE HOW TO MAKE THE WORLD A BETTER PLACE?

Shared Foundation: Explore
Featured Book: *Ada's Violin: The Story of the Recycled Orchestra of Paraguay* by Susan Hood

Summary

Can you imagine living in a town built upon a landfill? How can there be beauty and enjoyment with trash all around? After reading this inspiring story of creating beauty from a world full of trash, learners will be compelled to investigate how people make differences in each other's lives and the important role of music. Learners will have the opportunity to make their own music from recycled materials.

Pre-Assessment

- Pass out the "How Can People Make the World a Better Place?" worksheet (WS 5.1).
- Direct learners to circle "Pre-Assessment" next to their names.
- Ask learners to write and illustrate ideas about how people can make the world a better place.
- Assess understanding with the "Explore Create Competencies Rubric" (Appendix A.5).

> ★ *Learners will return to the same worksheet for a post-assessment, so be sure to save pre-assessments!*

THINK LESSON

Objective

Learners will consider how the orchestra in *Ada's Violin* impacted the larger community and the world beyond their own country.

AASL Standards Framework for Learners: V.A.1. Learners develop and satisfy personal curiosity by reading widely and deeply in multiple formats and write and create for a variety of purposes.

Lesson Duration

2 lessons, 60 minutes each

Materials

- Copy of *Ada's Violin: The Story of the Recycled Orchestra of Paraguay* by Susan Hood
- "*Ada's Violin*" anchor chart (AC 5.1)
- "Difference Makers" worksheet (WS 5.2)
- Pencils
- Computer lab
- Projector
- *Landfill Harmonic* (a Vimeo video with English subtitles)
- "Explore Think Competencies Rubric" (Appendix A.5)

Lesson Day 1

1. Tell learners that today they will hear the true story of a little girl whose world was forever changed because of one man's vision and the role of music.
2. Introduce *Ada's Violin: The Story of the Recycled Orchestra of Paraguay* by Susan Hood. Explain that this true story will lead to great investigations on the part of learners in the coming days.
3. Read the story aloud. Ask the following questions and write responses on the "*Ada's Violin*" anchor chart (AC 5.1):
   - "What is happening on the cover of the book?"
   - "What is the job of the people of Cateura? What is required by this job?" (p. 3)

ANCHOR CHART 5.1

 Ada's Violin

» A girl is playing a violin. She must be Ada. This story will be about Ada playing the violin. People are playing instruments on a hill of garbage. I wonder why?

» The people of Asunción pick through garbage to find things to recycle.

» The garbage must be really smelly. It seems very hot there.

» Music was a part of everyday life. Music made life beautiful.

» People are poor in Asunción and can't afford instruments.

» Favio Chávez started an orchestra with the children.

» Nícholás "Cola" Gómez made instruments with materials found in the dump.

» Favio Chávez kept the children out of trouble. He taught them to be disciplined musicians and to appreciate learning new things.

   – "What do you picture when you read the phrase 'noisy, stinking, sweltering slum'?" (p. 4)

   – "What influence did music have on Ada's family? How do you know?" (p. 7)

   – "What problem did Ada notice in her village? What examples of this problem can you find?" (p. 11)

   – "Why couldn't kids have real violins?" (p. 14)

   – "What solution did Favio Chávez come up with?" (p. 15)

   – "What materials were used to make instruments?" (p. 19)

   – "What character lessons did Favio Chávez teach the children?" (p. 22)

   – "Visualize Ada's first time on stage. What do you see?" (p. 27)

   – "How did the children's recycled orchestra solve a problem?" (p. 34)

4. Ask learners to think about how Favio Chávez made a difference. Pass out the "Difference Makers" worksheet (WS 5.2) and direct learners to answer the first question.

Lesson Day 2

1. Ask learners to share what they learned from the book *Ada's Violin: The Story of the Recycled Orchestra of Paraguay* by Susan Hood.

2. Explain that they will dive deeper into the Recycled Orchestra of Paraguay by watching *Landfill Harmonic*. Their job is to think about who the difference makers

are in the video and who those difference makers impacted. Choose "English CC" for English subtitles by clicking on the "CC" button on the bottom right corner of the video screen. Learners will respond to the second question on the "Difference Makers" worksheet (WS 5.2) after watching the video.

3. Assess learning with the "Explore Think Competencies Rubric" (Appendix A.5).

📌 *Would you like to see more video clips about this amazing project?*
A video search for the recycled orchestra will produce a movie trailer, links to a
documentary, and interviews.

CREATE LESSON

Objective
Learners will face challenges as they make instruments that create sound.

AASL Standards Framework for Learners: V.B.1. Learners construct new knowledge by problem solving through cycles of design, implementation, and reflection.

Lesson Duration
3 lessons, 45 minutes each

Materials
- "Sound Exploration" anchor chart (AC 5.2)
- Mobile devices
- Curated book resources about sound and musical instruments
- Traditional instruments with varying shapes
- Common objects that can create sound
- Cardboard
- Rubber bands
- Tin cans
- Recycled containers
- Plastic bottles
- Tape
- String
- Scissors
- Sticky notes
- "Planning Sheet" worksheet (Appendix B.1)
- "Explore Create Competencies Rubric" (Appendix A.5)

🚫 Sound Exploration

Name: _____

Recycled Item	Sound Item Makes	Feeling You Get from the Sound

Lesson Day 1

1. Tell learners that they will select a resource from the materials list to explore. They will name the instrument/item on a sticky note and add it to the grid on the "Sound Exploration" anchor chart (AC 5.2). On another sticky note, they will use adjectives to describe the sound that their instrument/item makes.

2. Explain that sounds often make people feel certain ways. Consider how the sounds of different instruments make students feel.

3. Add to the anchor chart as new instruments are considered.

Lesson Days 2 and 3

1. Prepare the room with a wide variety of materials that are easily visible and accessible.
2. Give learners the opportunity to hold and touch items to consider their sound quality.
3. Pass out the "Planning Sheet" worksheet (Appendix B.1) and ask learners to begin designing their instruments. Learners may begin building when their plan is set.
4. End the lesson period by having learners organize their work in a specific area or bin so it will be ready for the next day. Upon completion, learners should consider the sound that their instrument makes so they will be able to communicate this sound during the next lesson.
5. Assess learning with the "Explore Create Competencies Rubric" (Appendix A.5).

> 📌 *Find a location where you can leave items out for several days. Enlist the help of parent volunteers to coordinate the donation of recycled materials for the project. Also, consider providing a box or bin for each student to use to house materials he or she has gathered.*

SHARE LESSON

Objective
Learners will work together to create a collaborative piece of music to share with an audience.

AASL Standards Framework for Learners: V.C.3. Learners engage with the learning community by collaboratively identifying innovative solutions to a challenge or problem.

Lesson Duration
3–4 class sessions, 45–60 minutes each

Materials
- Student-created instruments
- Video/audio recording equipment
- "What We Learned about Making Instruments" anchor chart (AC 5.3)

- "Audience Feedback" worksheets (WS 5.3)
- Pencils
- "Explore Share Competencies Rubric" (Appendix A.5)

ANCHOR CHART 5.3

 What We Learned about Making Instruments

» Sound is made from a vibration.

» Each instrument needed a vibrating component.

» Working together and sharing ideas made the instruments better.

» It's fun exploring and creating sounds.

» We had to persevere when the instrument didn't work.

» We had to work around problems and try something new.

Lesson

1. Invite learners to share what they learned about making instruments. Record responses on the "What We Learned about Making Instruments" anchor chart (AC 5.3).
2. Ask learners to group themselves by the "sound" of their instrument. Allow them to highlight the sound and lead them in working in groups to develop a "song" that they will need to either record or be prepared to share live for their peers.
3. Explain that learners will share their learning and instruments with peers by performing (or sharing recorded music).
4. Instruct performers to ask their audiences for feedback by filling out the "Audience Feedback" worksheet (WS 5.3). Learners will reflect on how their music made their audience feel.
5. Assess progress with the "Explore Share Competencies Rubric" (Appendix A.5).

 GROW LESSON

Objective

Learners will create a project to share their learning outside the classroom.

AASL Standards Framework for Learners: V.D.2. Learners develop through experience and reflection by recognizing capabilities and skills that can be developed, improved, and expanded.

Lesson Duration

4 lessons, 60 minutes each

Materials

- Mobile devices with video/audio editing capability for recording
- Curated resources about recycling, Paraguay, instruments, music, and sound
- Art materials (markers, construction paper, etc.)
- Sticky notes
- Pencils
- Apps for creating content (*Seesaw*, *Tellagami*, *Kidblog*, and *Flipgrid*, all **AASL Best Apps for Teaching and Learning**)
- "Now What?" anchor chart (AC 5.4)
- "Explore Grow Competencies Rubric" (Appendix A.5)

ANCHOR CHART 5.4

Lesson Day 1

1. Ask learners, "How should we use our instruments to share our learning?" Prompt them to consider how they could make a difference in the greater school community through this work.
2. Invite learners to write ideas on sticky notes.
3. Place sticky notes on the "Now What?" anchor chart (AC 5.4). Arrange sticky notes by placing them in similar groups. Lead a conversation to determine a single project (or a couple of projects depending on comfort level).
4. Ask learners the following questions:
   - "Who will our audience be?"
   - "How will we appeal to them with our work?"
5. Create a list with learners of "next steps" for the next lesson.

Lesson Days 2 and 3

1. Set up spaces for small-group work. Distribute mobile devices, computer and reference materials, markers, construction paper, and any additional art materials you may have on hand.
2. Learners will begin collaborative work using their plans from the prior lesson and their instruments. This work will continue until a final product is achieved.

Lesson Day 4

1. Learners will consider how to promote their work through invitations, posters, signs, or newsletters.
2. Provide art materials for learners to create their presentations.
3. Allow time for learners to display their work and practice their presentations for peers. Determine how they should share.
4. Learners will present their work with a selected audience.
5. Assess work with the "Explore Grow Competencies Rubric" (Appendix A.5).

Post-Assessment

- Pass out the "How Can People Make the World a Better Place?" worksheet (WS 5.1) and read the directions.
- Direct learners to circle "Post-Assessment" next to their name.
- Assess understanding with the "Explore Create Competencies Rubric" (Appendix A.5).
- Compare results with the pre-assessment.

HOW CAN PEOPLE MAKE THE WORLD A BETTER PLACE?

Name: _____

Pre-Assessment/Post-Assessment

Directions: Write about how people can make the world a better place. Draw a picture to support your description.

_____

_____

_____

_____

_____

_____

DIFFERENCE MAKERS

Name: _____

After reading *Ada's Violin: The Story of the Recycled Orchestra of Paraguay* by Susan Hood, what did you learn about Favio Chávez? How did he make a difference? How did the orchestra make a difference?

_____

_____

_____

_____

_____

_____

Who are the difference makers in the video *Landfill Harmonic* (https://vimeo.com/ondemand/landfillharmonic/191085563)? Who did they impact?

_____

_____

_____

_____

_____

_____

AUDIENCE FEEDBACK

Group Name: _____

Directions: Ask audience members to answer the questions below after the performance.

What was the most interesting part of our performance?

_____

_____

_____

_____

What did you feel as you listened? Why?

_____

_____

_____

_____

What else do you want to know about recycled instruments?

_____

_____

_____

_____

HOW CAN PEOPLE IDENTIFY PROBLEMS?

Shared Foundation: Explore
Featured Book: *Follow the Moon Home:
A Tale of One Idea, Twenty Kids, and a Hundred
Sea Turtles* by Philippe Cousteau

Summary

Mother Earth does her best to take care of us, but now she needs our help. What problems exist in your backyard? What can you do to make a difference? *Follow the Moon Home: A Tale of One Idea, Twenty Kids, and a Hundred Sea Turtles* helps learners understand that they can make a difference. Readers follow a young girl as she rallies her community to help save baby sea turtles. The steps she takes to solve a relevant problem are memorable and easy to replicate. Engaging watercolor illustrations and colorful text make this how-to book an enjoyable read. Follow this mentor text to demonstrate the process of finding solutions to problems in your community.

Pre-Assessment

- Pass out the "Solving Community Problems" worksheet (WS 5.4).
- Ask learners to highlight or circle "Pre-Assessment" at the top of the worksheet.
- Assess knowledge with the "Explore Create Competencies Rubric" (Appendix A.5).

THINK LESSON

Objective

Learners will make observations in their community to realize problems that exist.

AASL Standards Framework for Learners: V.A.3. Learners develop and satisfy personal curiosity by engaging in inquiry-based processes for personal growth.

Lesson Duration

45–50 minutes

Materials

- Copy of *Follow the Moon Home: A Tale of One Idea, Twenty Kids, and a Hundred Sea Turtles* by Philippe Cousteau
- "How Vivienne Solved a Community Problem" anchor chart (AC 5.5)
- "Problems in My Community" worksheet (WS 5.5)
- Markers
- Pencils
- "Explore Think Competencies Rubric" (Appendix A.5)

★ *Enjoy discovering who the author's grandfather was by reading the "Letter to Young Activists" at the end of* Follow the Moon Home: A Tale of One Idea, Twenty Kids, and a Hundred Sea Turtles.

ANCHOR CHART 5.5

 How Vivienne Solved a Community Problem

Vivienne . . .

- » discovered a problem
- » asked a question
- » discussed solutions
- » made a plan
- » researched the problem
- » asked for help
- » informed the community

Lesson

1. Introduce the lesson by asking learners if they know of any animals that are in danger. What's happening to them? Explain that you will read a story about a girl who helps an animal in trouble. Read the title and the author of the book.
2. Say, "As I read, I would like you to pay attention to the steps the girl takes to make a difference."
3. Ask the following questions as you read *Follow the Moon Home: A Tale of One Idea, Twenty Kids, and a Hundred Sea Turtles* by Philippe Cousteau.
    - "What do you notice about the anchor chart in the book?" (p. 3)
    - "How does Vivienne look for problems?" (p. 5)
    - "What question does Vivienne ask on this page? Why is this important?" (p. 11)

– "What's happening on these pages? What should we pay attention to?" (pp. 13–16)
– "What has happened so far?" (p. 26)
– "Was Vivienne successful? Why do you think that?" (p. 34)

4. Challenge learners to remember all the steps Vivienne took to save baby sea turtles. Write the process on the "How Vivienne Solved a Community Problem" anchor chart (AC 5.5).
5. Invite learners to think about problems in their communities. Pass out the "Problems in My Community" worksheet (WS 5.5). Tell learners that they will carry their worksheet with them for the next week. Instruct them to look for problems wherever they go and make note of them. Ask them to write any questions they have about the problems they discover.
6. Assess responses with the "Explore Think Competencies Rubric" (Appendix A.5).

CREATE LESSON

Objective
Learners will work together and implement a plan that draws attention to a community problem.

AASL Standards Framework for Learners: V.B.1. Learners construct new knowledge by problem solving through cycles of design, implementation, and reflection.

Lesson Duration
45–50 minutes

Materials
- "Problems in My Community" worksheet (WS 5.5) from previous lesson
- Dry erase board
- Dry erase markers
- "Group Interaction" anchor chart (AC 3.5)
- "Problem-Solving Planning Sheet" worksheet (WS 5.6)
- Pencils
- "Planning Exit Slip" (WS 5.7)
- "Explore Create Competencies Rubric" (Appendix A.5)

Lesson

1. Ask learners to share some of the problems they noticed in their neighborhoods. Record ideas on a dry erase board.
2. Explain that learners will work with a group to choose a problem to solve. They will develop a plan to solve it.
3. Ask learners to share tips for group work. Record ideas on the "Group Interaction" anchor chart (AC 3.5).
4. Form groups of learners and pass out the "Problem-Solving Planning Sheet" worksheet (WS 5.6).
5. Tell learners to fill out a "Planning Exit Slip" (WS 5.7) when they are done with their plans.
6. Assess learning with the "Explore Create Competencies Rubric" (Appendix A.5).

SHARE LESSON

Objective
Learners will identify sources to investigate community problems.

AASL Standards Framework for Learners: V.C.2. Learners engage with the learning community by co-constructing innovative means of investigation.

Lesson Duration
45–50 minutes

Materials
- "Investigate" anchor chart (AC 5.6)
- Markers
- *Padlet,* an **AASL Best Website for Teaching and Learning**
- "Interview Exit Ticket" worksheet (WS 5.8)
- Pencils
- Computer lab
- Mobile devices
- "Explore Share Competencies Rubric" (Appendix A.5)

 Prepare separate Padlets for each group ahead of time. Share the links for each Padlet on your library website for easy access.

Investigate

How will you learn more about the problem in your community?

» Read local news.

» Interview people.

» Send e-mails.

» Write letters.

» Search for reliable information.

Lesson

1. Invite learners to share some of their plans to solve community problems.
2. Ask, "How can we find out more about these problems?" Record responses on the "Investigate" anchor chart (AC 5.6).
3. Ask, "If you could interview someone to learn more about your problem, who would it be? What would you ask that person?" Explain that learners will post their questions to the people they want to interview on an online social platform. The person they direct the questions to will be invited to respond on the platform. With a link to the platform, anyone can read and respond to posts.
4. Demonstrate how to access the different Padlets. Show learners how to post a question. Tell learners to write their initials on their posts.
5. Explain that you will send an e-mail to people who could answer their questions. Learners can access the link to the Padlet to see if the questions were answered.
6. Discuss what needs to be in a sentence with a question. Model how to type a question mark and an uppercase letter.
7. Ask learners to complete the "Interview Exit Ticket" (WS 5.8) after their questions are answered on the Padlets.
8. Assess learning with the "Explore Share Competencies Rubric" (Appendix A.5).

 ## GROW LESSON

Objective

Learners will begin to implement their plan by assigning jobs to group members.

AASL Standards Framework for Learners: V.D.2. Learners develop through experience and reflection by recognizing capabilities and skills that can be developed, improved, and expanded.

Lesson Duration

45–50 minutes

Materials
- "Call to Action" anchor chart (AC 5.7)
- Markers
- "Friends Working Together" worksheet (WS 5.9)
- Pencils
- "Explore Grow Competencies Rubric" (Appendix A.5)

 Call to Action

How did Vivienne recruit help and inform her community?
- » She invited experts to speak.
- » She made and distributed posters.
- » She wrote fact sheets.
- » She raised money with a bake sale.
- » She asked for donations.
- » She alerted the press.
- » She invited enthusiasts to see her presentation.

Lesson
1. Review with learners how Vivienne informed the community about the sea turtle problem and asked for help. Turn to the pages that demonstrate Vivienne taking action in *Follow the Moon Home: A Tale of One Idea, Twenty Kids, and a Hundred Sea Turtles.* List her steps on the "Call to Action" anchor chart (AC 5.7).
2. Ask learners how they would like to inform the community about their problem. Explain that they will name different jobs they can do to remedy the problem. Each group will assign appropriate jobs to group members.
3. Pass out the "Friends Working Together" worksheet (WS 5.9).
4. Save responses to assess learning with the "Explore Grow Competencies Rubric" (Appendix A.5).

Post-Assessment
- Pass out the "Solving Community Problems" worksheet (WS 5.4).
- Direct learners to circle the word "Post-Assessment" at the top of the page to distinguish this from the initial assessment.
- Assess knowledge with the "Explore Create Competencies Rubric" (Appendix A.5).
- Compare results with the pre-assessment.

SOLVING COMMUNITY PROBLEMS

Name: _____

Pre-Assessment/Post-Assessment

What do you need to solve a problem in your community?

- _____

- _____

- _____

- _____

- _____

- _____

- _____

- _____

- _____

- _____

- _____

- _____

- _____

- _____

- _____

PROBLEMS IN MY COMMUNITY

Name:

Problems I See	Questions I Have

PROBLEM-SOLVING PLANNING SHEET

Names of Group Members:

- _____   • _____

- _____   • _____

- _____   • _____

Describe the problem:

_____

_____

_____

How will you research the problem?

_____

_____

What is your plan to solve the problem?

1) _____

2) _____

3) _____

What do you need to solve your problem?

- _____

- _____

- _____

PLANNING EXIT SLIP

Name: _____

Explain how you helped develop a plan to solve a problem.

_____

_____

_____

_____

_____

_____

_____

- -

PLANNING EXIT SLIP

Name: _____

Explain how you helped develop a plan to solve a problem.

_____

_____

_____

_____

_____

_____

INTERVIEW EXIT TICKET

Name:

How does using *Padlet* help me find answers to my questions?

_____

_____

_____

- -

Name:

How does using *Padlet* help me find answers to my questions?

_____

_____

_____

- -

Name:

How does using *Padlet* help me find answers to my questions?

_____

_____

_____

FRIENDS WORKING TOGETHER

Names of Group Members:

- _____
- _____
- _____
- _____
- _____
- _____

Directions: In the first column, list the jobs that need to get done in order to fix the problem. In the middle column, assign a group member to each job. List the person's skills in the third column.

Jobs That Need to Get Done to Fix the Problem	The Best Person for the Job	What Skills Does This Person Have?

HOW CAN PEOPLE FIND SOLUTIONS TO PROBLEMS IN THEIR COMMUNITY?

Shared Foundation: Explore
Featured Book: *One Plastic Bag: Isatou Ceesay and the Recycling Women of the Gambia* by Miranda Paul

Summary

Imagine living in a place where there was no trash pick-up and no dump. What would you do with your garbage? If you lived in Njau, Gambia, you would leave your trash on the road. This is not healthy, especially for the goats who die from eating discarded plastic bags. Isatou Ceesay is fixing this problem. With a great deal of ingenuity and help from her friends, she found a way to reinvent plastic bags. This true story will inspire readers to think about the environmental impact plastic bags are making in their community. Learners will be compelled to change the way they carry their food after reading this inspiring story.

Pre-Assessment

- Pass out the "Solving Community Problems" worksheet (WS 5.4).
- Ask learners to highlight or circle "Pre-Assessment" at the top of the worksheet.
- Assess with the "Explore Create Competencies Rubric" (Appendix A.5).

THINK LESSON

Objective

Learners will investigate questions they have about plastic.

AASL Standards Framework for Learners: V.A.3. Learners develop and satisfy personal curiosity by engaging in inquiry-based processes for personal growth.

Lesson Duration

50–60 minutes

Materials

- A copy of *One Plastic Bag: Isatou Ceesay and the Recycling Women of the Gambia* by Miranda Paul
- "Plastic KWL Chart" anchor chart (AC 5.8)

- Markers
- *Wonderopolis,* an **AASL Best Website for Teaching and Learning**
- Projector
- Computer lab or mobile devices
- Sticky notes
- Pencils
- "Explore Think Competencies Rubric" (Appendix A.5)

ANCHOR CHART 5.8

Plastic KWL Chart

I Know . . .	I Wonder . . .	I Learned . . .

Lesson

1. Engage learners by asking them what they do with used plastic bags. Explain that some people get creative with plastic bags and think of new ways to use them.
2. Introduce *One Plastic Bag: Isatou Ceesay and the Recycling Women of the Gambia*. Point out that this is a true story about a woman who reuses plastic bags to solve a problem.
3. Ask the following questions as you read the story:
   - "What can you infer about Njau, Gambia, after reading the first two pages and observing the illustrations?" (pp. 1–2)
   - "What did you learn about Isatou's bag that broke?" (p. 4)
   - "What can you infer about the meaning of the word *mbuba*?" (p. 5)
   - "What questions do you have after reading this page?" (p. 9)
   - "What question does Isatou ask on this page? Why is it important?" (p. 15)
   - "What words would you use to describe Isatou?" (p. 20)
4. Invite learners to share what they know about plastic. Write responses on the "Plastic KWL Chart" anchor chart (AC 5.8).
5. Ask learners what they wonder about plastic. Write questions on the "Plastic KWL Chart" anchor chart (AC 5.8).
6. Invite learners to search for the word *plastic* on *Wonderopolis*. Instruct them to read the information about plastic to find answers to their questions. Tell learners to write what they learned about plastic on a sticky note and include their name. Invite them to place the sticky note on the "Plastic KWL Chart" anchor chart (AC 5.8). Review some of the sticky notes together at the end of the class.
7. Assess responses on sticky notes with the "Explore Think Competencies Rubric" (Appendix A.5).

CREATE LESSON

Objective
Learners will find new ways to use plastic bags.

AASL Standards Framework for Learners: V.B.2. Learners construct new knowledge by persisting through self-directed pursuits by tinkering and making.

Lesson Duration
2 lessons, 45–50 minutes each

Materials

- Copy of *The Most Magnificent Thing* by Ashley Spires
- "Perseverance" anchor chart (AC 5.9)
- Plastic bags
- *DIY,* an **AASL Best Website for Teaching and Learning**
- Computer lab or mobile devices
- "Planning Sheet" (Appendix B.1)
- "Explore Create Competencies Rubric" (Appendix A.5)

ANCHOR CHART 5.9

Perseverance

What Perseverance Looks Like
- » Trying different ideas
- » Asking for help
- » Taking a break when stuck
- » Sticking with it
- » Not giving up
- » Taking deep breaths when feeling frustrated

What Perseverance Does Not Look Like
- » Quitting
- » Giving up
- » Banging things
- » Not trying

Lesson Day 1

1. Introduce the lesson by saying, "Think of a time when you struggled making something. What was it? What happened? Today, we are going to read a story about a little girl who runs into a problem while building an idea. While I read, pay close attention to how she handles the problem."
2. Ask, "How did she handle the problem? Why is that important? What does it look like to persevere through challenges?" Write responses on the "Perseverance" anchor chart (AC 5.9).
3. Inform learners that they will take what they learned about perseverance and make something out of plastic bags. They will visit the *DIY* website and search for "plastic bags" to generate ideas.
4. Pass out the "Planning Sheet" worksheet (Appendix B.1). Instruct learners to develop a plan to create something useful out of plastic bags.
5. Review the material lists with learners. Send a note to parents and other educators asking for donations.

Lesson Day 2

1. Review what it looks like and sounds like to persevere before learners start making their plastic creations. Offer guidance and support as needed throughout the making process.
2. Assess learning while learners create using the "Explore Create Competencies Rubric" (Appendix A.5).

SHARE LESSON

Objective

Learners will investigate the recycling process and share their knowledge with other classes and their community.

AASL Standards Framework for Learners: V.C.1. Learners engage with the learning community by expressing curiosity about a topic of personal interest or curricular relevance.

Lesson Duration

2 lessons, 45–50 minutes each

Materials

- Representative from the local recycling center
- "Recycling KWL Chart" anchor chart (AC 5.10)
- "Group Work" anchor chart (AC 2.9)
- Markers
- "Presentation Plan" worksheet (WS 3.4)
- Mobile devices with movie app
- Mobile devices with e-book creator app
- Posterboards
- Markers
- Crayons
- Pencils
- "Explore Share Competencies Rubric" (Appendix A.5)

⭐ *Invite a representative from the local recycling center to the lesson. If the individual can't make it in person, perhaps she or he would consider video chatting or responding to questions through e-mail.*

Recycling KWL Chart

I Know . . .	I Wonder . . .	I Learned . . .

Lesson Day 1

1. Ask learners what they know about recycling. Invite questions about recycling. Write responses on the "Recycling KWL Chart" anchor chart (AC 5.10).
2. Invite a representative from the local recycling center to answer the questions. Record answers on the "Recycling KWL Chart" anchor chart (AC 5.10).
3. Tell learners that they will create posters, videos, and e-books to inform other classes about recycling. Today they will work in groups to plan a presentation. They will use the "Presentation Plan" worksheet (WS 3.4) to help them organize their ideas. Form groups of learners and pass out the "Presentation Plan" worksheet (WS 3.4).

ANCHOR CHART 5.11

 Presentations

What makes a good video?

- Close-up shots
- Still camera
- Loud, clear voice
- Clear directions

What makes a good e-book?

- Close-up shots
- Clear pictures
- Easy-to-follow steps with numbers or bullet points
- Labels
- Diagrams
- Clear directions

What makes a good poster?

- Limited amount of words
- Clear, direct steps
- Labels
- Diagrams

It might be worthwhile to spend time noticing what makes a good video, e-book, and poster. Share good and bad examples found on the Internet, and ask learners to give feedback.

Lesson Day 2

1. Invite learners to share some of their presentation ideas. Discuss what it looks like and sounds like to work together to create a project.
2. Discuss what makes a good presentation. Write responses on the "Presentations" anchor chart (AC 5.11).

3. Pass out the "Presentation Plan" worksheet (WS 3.4) from the previous lesson. Ask one person from each group to gather supplies. Learners can begin working on their presentations.
4. Assess the "Presentation Plan" worksheets (WS 3.4) with the "Explore Share Competencies Rubric" (Appendix A.5).

GROW LESSON

Objective
Learners will present their movies and posters and ask for feedback.

AASL Standards Framework for Learners: V.D.3. Learners develop through experience and reflection by open-mindedly accepting feedback for positive and constructive growth.

Lesson Duration
45–50 minutes

Materials
- Presentations from previous lesson
- "Feedback Sentence Starters" anchor chart (AC 1.15)
- Markers
- "Constructive Feedback" slip (WS 1.9)
- "Reflecting on Feedback" worksheet (WS 5.10)
- Pencils
- "Explore Grow Competencies Rubric" (Appendix A.5)

Lesson
1. Inform learners that they will present their work to the classroom and ask for feedback. Explain that they will reflect on the feedback and consider making changes to their presentations. Ask why feedback is helpful.
2. Model what giving feedback looks like by following the starter sentences on the "Feedback Sentence Starters" anchor chart (AC 1.15).
3. Explain that the audience will fill out a "Constructive Feedback" slip (WS 1.9) for each group.
4. Collect the "Constructive Feedback" slips (WS 1.9) after the presentations and distribute them to the presenters.

5. Groups will discuss the feedback and consider making changes. Each group will record members' thinking on the "Reflecting on Feedback" worksheets (WS 5.10).

6. Assess the "Reflecting on Feedback" worksheet (WS 5.10) with the "Explore Grow Competencies Rubric" (Appendix A.5).

Post-Assessment

- Pass out the "Solving Community Problems" worksheet (WS 5.4).
- Ask learners to circle the word "Post-Assessment" at the top of the page to distinguish this from the initial assessment.
- Assess progress using the "Explore Create Competencies Rubric" (Appendix A.5).
- Compare results with the pre-assessment.

REFLECTING ON FEEDBACK

Names of Team Members:

- _____   - _____

- _____   - _____

What ideas were helpful?

_____

_____

_____

What changes will you make?

_____

_____

_____

Why is feedback important?

_____

_____

_____

_____

WHY IS IT IMPORTANT TO FIND INNOVATIVE SOLUTIONS TO PROBLEMS?

Shared Foundation: Explore
Featured Book: *Farmer Will Allen and the Growing Table* by Jacqueline Briggs Martin

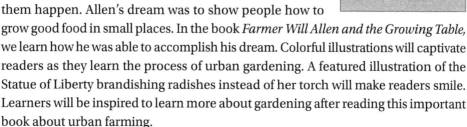

Summary

What does it mean to be innovative? If you are Farmer Will Allen, innovation means seeing possibilities and making them happen. Allen's dream was to show people how to grow good food in small places. In the book *Farmer Will Allen and the Growing Table*, we learn how he was able to accomplish his dream. Colorful illustrations will captivate readers as they learn the process of urban gardening. A featured illustration of the Statue of Liberty brandishing radishes instead of her torch will make readers smile. Learners will be inspired to learn more about gardening after reading this important book about urban farming.

Pre-Assessment
- Distribute the "Innovator" worksheet (WS 5.11).
- Ask learners to highlight or circle "Pre-Assessment" at the top of the worksheet.
- Assess understanding with the "Explore Create Competencies Rubric" (Appendix A.5).

THINK LESSON

Objective
Learners will investigate vermicomposting.

AASL Standards Framework for Learners: V.A.3. Learners develop and satisfy personal curiosity by engaging in inquiry-based processes for personal growth.

Lesson Duration
50 minutes

Materials
- "How Is Farmer Will Allen an Innovator?" anchor chart (AC 5.12)
- Markers
- "Questions I Have about Vermicomposting" worksheet (WS 5.12)

- Pencils
- *Vermicomposting: How Worms Can Reduce Our Waste,* a TED-Ed video
- Projector
- Computer or mobile device
- "Explore Think Competencies Rubric" (Appendix A.5)

How Is Farmer Will Allen an Innovator?

- He sees things differently.
- He finds solutions to problems.
- He asks for help.
- He shares his knowledge.
- He makes a difference.

Lesson

1. Introduce the lesson by defining the word *innovator* as a person who introduces new methods, ideas, or products. Ask learners if they can name an innovative person. What makes that person innovative?
2. Say, "Today I am going to read a book about an innovative farmer. His name is Will Allen. Let's find out what he does that makes him innovative. When you see an example of innovation in the book, raise your hand. We'll make note of it on our 'How Is Farmer Will Allen an Innovator?' anchor chart" (AC 5.12).
3. Ask the following questions as you read the book:
   - "What did you learn about Farmer Will Allen on this page?" (p. 1)
   - "What is important to Farmer Will Allen? How do you know?" (p. 3)
   - "What is Farmer Will Allen doing on this page? Why is it important?" (p. 8)
   - "What problem did Farmer Will Allen face? How did he solve it?" (p. 10)
   - "What did you learn about red wigglers?" (pp. 11–14)
   - "What is Farmer Will Allen doing on this page? Why is it important?" (p. 15)
   - "Why is sharing knowledge important?" (p. 20)
   - "What is Farmer Will Allen's message?" (p. 22)

4. Revisit the pages that explain the importance of worms in gardening (pp. 11–14).
5. Watch *Vermicomposting: How Worms Can Reduce Our Waste,* a TED-Ed video.
6. Inform learners that they will be challenged to design and build their own vermicomposting bin. What questions do they have about vermicomposting before they start planning? Pass out the "Questions I Have about Vermicomposting" worksheet (WS 5.12).
7. Assess questions with the "Explore Think Competencies Rubric" (Appendix A.5).

CREATE LESSON

Objective
Learners will be challenged to design and build a vermicomposting container.

AASL Standards Framework for Learners: V.B.2. Learners construct new knowledge by persisting through self-directed pursuits by tinkering and making.

Lesson Duration
2 lessons, 50–60 minutes each

Materials
- "What Do We Notice?" anchor chart (AC 5.13)
- Markers
- Pencils
- Volunteers
- Materials to make indoor worm bins
    - Red wiggler worms
    - Plastic containers with lids
    - Soil
    - Paper
    - Food scraps
    - Drill
    - Safety goggles
    - Water
- "Innovative Worm Bin Design" worksheet (WS 5.13)
- "Explore Create Competencies Rubric" (Appendix A.5)

ANCHOR CHART 5.13

 What Do We Notice?

What do you notice about vermicomposting bins?
- » Most are plastic.
- » There are holes in the lid.
- » There are leaves and soil in the bin.

★ *Making vermicomposting bins will get messy. Bring the lesson outdoors where spills won't matter.*

Lesson Day 1

1. Introduce the lesson by asking learners to remind you of what makes Farmer Will Allen innovative. Ask learners what skills they need to be innovative.
2. Explain that today they will work in groups to design an innovative vermicomposting bin for classrooms. Say, "Let's look at some examples to think about what we need to build our own indoor worm composting bin."
3. Search for "indoor worm bins" or "vermicomposting" images. Ask learners what they notice. Record answers on the "What Do We Notice?" anchor chart (AC 5.13).
4. Form groups of learners. Pass out the "Innovative Worm Bin Design" worksheet (WS 5.13). Review the list of needed materials and send letters to educators and parents asking for material donations.

Lesson Day 2

1. Begin building vermicomposting bins. Offer guidance and support. Adults will be in charge of the drill.
2. Assess work as you listen in on conversations and monitor behaviors. Use the "Explore Create Competencies Rubric" to record observations (Appendix A.5).

SHARE LESSON

Objective

Learners will explain how to maintain the vermicomposting bins and ask for regular feedback.

AASL Standards Framework for Learners: V.C.3. Learners engage with the learning community by collaboratively identifying innovative solutions to a challenge or problem.

Lesson Duration

45–50 minutes

Materials

- "Questions Learners May Have" anchor chart (AC 5.14)
- Markers
- Paper
- Crayons
- Pencils
- "Explore Share Competencies Rubric" (Appendix A.5)

ANCHOR CHART 5.14

 Questions Learners May Have

» What is a vermicomposting bin?

» Why is it in our classroom?

» What do we have to do to take care of it?

» What do we do if we have questions?

» Will it smell?

» Will the worms get out?

» Why should we care?

Lesson

1. Discuss what students learned while making their vermicomposting bins. Explain that it's time for them to share what they learned with other classes. They are going to donate their bin to a class and explain what it is and how to maintain it. They will visit the class regularly to monitor the bin and ask for feedback.

2. Ask, "What questions can we anticipate from students about the vermicomposting bins you are donating to their classrooms?" Write responses on the "Questions Learners May Have" anchor chart (AC 5.14).

3. Explain that learners will practice demonstrating the purpose of their bins and how to take care of them. They will create feedback slips to leave in classrooms. All bins will be visited regularly, and the feedback slips will be reviewed.

4. Monitor demonstrations and review feedback slips to assess learning with the "Explore Share Competencies Rubric" (Appendix A.5).

GROW LESSON

Objective

Learners will maintain their vermicomposting bins and make necessary adjustments.

AASL Standards Framework for Learners: V.D.3. Learners develop through experience and reflection by open-mindedly accepting feedback for positive and constructive growth.

Lesson Duration

45–50 minutes

Materials
- "Vermicomposting Presentations" anchor chart (AC 5.15)
- Markers
- "Explore Grow Competencies Rubric" (Appendix A.5)

Lesson
1. Ask learners how they are feeling about their demonstrations. Explain that today they will prepare for classroom presentations by practicing in front of their peers and asking for feedback.
2. Record feedback on the "Vermicomposting Presentations" anchor chart (AC 5.15).
3. Release learners to discuss any changes with their group.
4. Monitor discussions and assess learning with the "Explore Grow Competencies Rubric" (Appendix A.5).

Post-Assessment
- Distribute the "Innovator" worksheet (WS 5.11).
- Ask learners to circle the word "Post-Assessment" at the top of the page to distinguish this from the initial assessment.
- Assess understanding with the "Explore Create Competencies Rubric" (Appendix A.5).
- Compare results with the pre-assessment.

🚫 Vermicomposting Presentations

Group 1

Ideas and comments from the audience

» _____

» _____

» _____

Group 2

Ideas and comments from the audience

» _____

» _____

» _____

Group 3

Ideas and comments from the audience

» _____

» _____

» _____

Group 4

Ideas and comments from the audience

» _____

» _____

» _____

INNOVATOR

Name: _____

Pre-Assessment/Post-Assessment

What does an innovator do?

QUESTIONS I HAVE ABOUT VERMICOMPOSTING

Name: _____

I wonder _____

_____

I wonder _____

_____

I wonder _____

_____

I wonder _____

_____

I wonder _____

_____

I wonder _____

_____

I wonder _____

_____

INNOVATIVE WORM BIN DESIGN

Names of Group Members:

- _____   • _____

- _____   • _____

- _____   • _____

Design Challenge: Innovate an indoor worm bin that would work well in a classroom setting.

> Design Idea:
>
>
>
>
>
>
>
>
>
>
>
>

List of Needed Materials:

- _____

- _____

- _____

How Will We Get the Materials?

_____

_____

_____

CHAPTER 6

Engage Lessons

KEY COMMITMENT
Demonstrate safe, legal, and ethical creating and sharing of knowledge products independently while engaging in a community of practice and an interconnected world.

HOW DOES OUR BACKGROUND INFLUENCE PERCEPTION?

Shared Foundation: Engage
Featured Book: *They All Saw a Cat*
by Brendan Wenzel

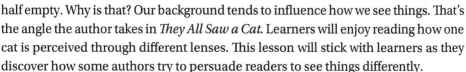

Summary
You are familiar with the glass half full adage, right? Well, some people see that same glass as half empty. Why is that? Our background tends to influence how we see things. That's the angle the author takes in *They All Saw a Cat*. Learners will enjoy reading how one cat is perceived through different lenses. This lesson will stick with learners as they discover how some authors try to persuade readers to see things differently.

Pre-Assessment
- Pass out the "Author's Purpose" worksheet (WS 6.1).
- Ask learners to highlight or circle "Pre-Assessment" at the top of the worksheet.
- Assess understanding with the "Engage Think Competencies Rubric" (Appendix A.6).

THINK LESSON

Objective
Learners will consider how authors want readers to feel about a topic by studying the words and the pictures.

AASL Standards Framework for Learners: VI.A.3. Learners follow ethical and legal guidelines for gathering and using information by evaluating information for accuracy, validity, social and cultural context, and appropriateness for need.

Lesson Duration
45–50 minutes

Materials
- Copy of *They All Saw a Cat* by Brendan Wenzel
- Collection of bat books, some with scary images of bats
- Copy of *Stellaluna* by Janell Cannon
- Collection of animal books, enough for every learner
- "Author's Perception about Bats" anchor chart (AC 6.1)
- "Question Exit Slip" worksheet (WS 6.2)
- "Engage Think Competencies Rubric" (Appendix A.6)

ANCHOR CHART 6.1

⊘ Author's Perception about Bats

Title of Book: Author's Name:	Author's Perception:
Title of Book: Author's Name:	Author's Perception:
Title of Book: Author's Name:	Author's Perception:
Title of Book: Author's Name:	Author's Perception:
Title of Book: Author's Name:	Author's Perception:

Lesson

1. Introduce the lesson by asking learners the following questions:
   - "How do you feel about bats?"
   - "What words would you use to describe a bat?"
   - "If you were to illustrate bats for a book, what would the bats look like?"

2. Read the title of the book and mention that it is a Caldecott Honor book. Ask, "When we see a Caldecott Honor Medal on the cover of a picture book, what can we expect?"

3. Ask learners to think about how differently people and animals view bats as you read the book. At the end of the story, give more examples of perception, using bees and peanuts as examples. Some people are afraid of these things because of serious allergies or a bad experience. Explain that many authors see things differently, too. Hold up a pile of bat books. Show the covers of the books. Ask learners to think about how the authors feel about bats by looking at the covers of their books. Hold up a copy of *Stellaluna*. Ask learners how they think Janell Cannon feels about bats. Write responses on the "Author's Perception about Bats" anchor chart (AC 6.1).

4. Explain that we all have different perceptions of things, and it's important to remember that authors do, too. Say, "Understanding this will help us realize that we should read more than one book to get a balanced perspective on a topic."

5. Invite learners to look at some of the animal books. Ask, "What is the author's perspective of their featured animal? Why does their perspective matter?"

6. Pass out the "Question Exit Slip" worksheet (WS 6.2).

7. Assess questions with the "Engage Think Competencies Rubric" (Appendix A.6).

CREATE LESSON

Objective

Learners will collect examples of persuasive pictures in books and cite the authors' information.

AASL Standards Framework for Learners: VI.B.2. Learners use valid information and reasoned conclusions to make ethical decisions in the creation of knowledge by acknowledging authorship and demonstrating respect for the intellectual property of others.

Lesson Duration

45–50 minutes

Materials

- "Book Citation" anchor chart (AC 6.2)
- *Seesaw* app, an **AASL Best App for Teaching and Learning**
- Collection of animal books, enough for every learner
- Mobile devices
- "Engage Create Competencies Rubric" (Appendix A.6)

> ★ *Collect animal books with scary and cute pictures. Find examples of different perspectives for each animal.*

ANCHOR CHART 6.2

 Book Citation

Last Name, First Name. Book Title.

EXAMPLE: Wenzel, Brendan. *They All Saw a Cat.*

Why is it important to mention the name of the author?
  » Taking someone's idea without giving credit is stealing.
  » People will think it is your idea when it's not.
  » The author will appreciate the mention.
  » It is respectful.

> ★ *The citation form for this lesson requires only the basic information for young learners. The anchor chart asks learners to mention only the book title and the author.*

Lesson

1. Introduce the lesson by asking learners the following questions:
   - "When you make something or write something in school, you are always reminded to put your name on your work. Why is that?"
   - "How would you feel if someone took your work and put her name on it?"

2. Explain that every time learners borrow information from a book for a report, they should write the name of the author and the title of the book. This way, the author gets credit for his work.

3. Demonstrate how to write a basic citation using *They All Saw a Cat* as a model. Write the citation on the "Book Citation" anchor chart (AC 6.2).
4. Explain that learners are going to find an example of a book that is trying to persuade the reader to feel a certain way. They will use the *Seesaw* app to take a picture of their example. Demonstrate how to use the drawing tool to highlight the persuasive features. Model writing a basic citation with the text tool.
5. Assess work with the "Engage Create Competencies Rubric" (Appendix A.6).

SHARE LESSON

Objective
Learners will write a book review using the online catalog or *Bookopolis*.

AASL Standards Framework for Learners: VI.C.2. Learners responsibly, ethically, and legally share new information with a global community by disseminating new knowledge through means appropriate for the intended audience.

Lesson Duration
45–50 minutes

Materials
- "Reviewing Illustrations" anchor chart (AC 6.3)
- Animal books from previous lesson
- *Bookopolis,* an **AASL Best Website for Teaching and Learning**
- Computer lab or mobile devices
- "Engage Share Competencies Rubric" (Appendix A.6)

ANCHOR CHART 6.3

 Reviewing Illustrations

» Describe the colors.
» Describe the medium (chalk, watercolor, paint, etc.).
» "The pictures will compel you to . . . "
» "If you like horses, you'll love these illustrations!"
» "If you are afraid of mice, you might want to pass on this scary book about rodents."

📌 *Does your online catalog allow learners to write book reviews? If so, use your online catalog for this lesson.*

Lesson

1. Ask learners what they think about the animal books they have been reading. Explain that today they will write a review about their books using *Bookopolis.*
2. Explain that their reviews will include a description of the illustrations. Point out that their reviews will be online, so they should be mindful of what they post. Remind them that anyone can read what they write, including the authors.
3. Model what it looks like to review an illustration. Go through the points listed on the "Reviewing Illustrations" anchor chart (AC 6.3).
4. Model how to access *Bookopolis* and write a review.
5. Assess reviews using the "Engage Share Competencies Rubric" (Appendix A.6).

GROW LESSON

Objective

Learners will explore safe places to find copyright-free images.

AASL Standards Framework for Learners: VI.D.1. Learners engage with information to extend personal learning by personalizing their use of information and information technologies.

Lesson Duration

40–50 minutes

Materials

- *Pixabay,* an **AASL Best Website for Teaching and Learning**
- *Photos for Class,* an **AASL Best Website for Teaching and Learning**
- Computer lab or mobile devices
- "Images for Projects" anchor chart (AC 6.4)
- Markers
- Copy of *They All Saw a Cat* by Brendan Wenzel
- "Image Citation" worksheet (WS 6.3)
- Pencils
- "Engage Grow Competencies Rubric" (Appendix A.6)

Images for Projects

What images can I use for a project?
  » *Pixabay* (https://pixabay.com/)
  » *Photos for Class* (www.photosforclass.com/)

What is copyright?
  » When you make something, people can't copy it unless they ask for your permission.

What is royalty free?
  » You don't have to pay a fee to use the picture.

Lesson

1. Invite learners to discuss what they have learned so far about looking at pictures in books. Why is it important to understand how the author feels about a topic?
2. Hold up a copy of *They All Saw a Cat* by Brendan Wenzel. Remind learners that at the beginning of the unit, they were asked how they felt about cats. Explain that today they get to show how they feel about cats or any animal of their choice. They will go to royalty-free and copyright-free websites to find images about an animal.
3. Define the words *royalty* and *copyright.* Record definitions on the "Images for Projects" anchor chart (AC 6.4). Explain that *Pixabay* and *Photos for Class* are websites that they can use to find copyright- and royalty-free images. Model how to search for images on the websites. Explain that learners can use any of the photos they find but that they should mention in their work the title of the image and the website where the image was found.
4. Pass out the "Image Citation" worksheet (WS 6.3).
5. Assess responses with the "Engage Grow Competencies Rubric" (Appendix A.6).

Post-Assessment

- Pass out the "Author's Purpose" worksheet (WS 6.1).
- Ask learners to circle the word "Post-Assessment" at the top of the page to distinguish this from the initial assessment.
- Assess understanding with the "Engage Think Competencies Rubric" (Appendix A.6).
- Compare results with the pre-assessment to assess growth.

AUTHOR'S PURPOSE

Name: _____

Pre-Assessment/Post-Assessment

Why is it important to understand how the author feels about a topic?

_____

_____

_____

_____

_____

_____

_____

_____

_____

_____

_____

_____

_____

_____

WORKSHEET 6.2

QUESTION EXIT SLIP

TICKET
ADMIT ONE

Name: _____

What question should you consider when reading nonfiction?

_____

_____

_____

QUESTION EXIT SLIP

TICKET
ADMIT ONE

Name: _____

What question should you consider when reading nonfiction?

_____

_____

_____

QUESTION EXIT SLIP

TICKET
ADMIT ONE

Name: _____

What question should you consider when reading nonfiction?

_____

_____

_____

WORKSHEET 6.3

IMAGE CITATION

Name: ______________________________

Image 1

Does the image have a title? **YES** **NO**

If yes, what is the title of the image?

____

What is the name of the website where you found your image?

____

What is the web address?

____

Image 2

Does the image have a title? **YES** **NO**

If yes, what is the title of the image?

____

What is the name of the website where you found your image?

____

What is the web address?

____

WHAT CAUSES PEOPLE TO HAVE CERTAIN FEELINGS ABOUT DIFFERENT ANIMALS?

Shared Foundation: Engage
Featured Book: *Fox's Garden*
by Princesse Camcam

Summary

If you saw a fox on a cold winter night, what would you do? Would you shoo the critter away or let it be? In *Fox's Garden,* the author invites us to join a little boy as he carefully observes the fox and takes care of her. The wordless book engages the reader with creative illustrations fashioned in paper doll cutouts. It tells the story of having compassion for a creature that often gets a bad reputation. Learners will be compelled to establish a new understanding of the wild fox.

Pre-Assessment

- Pass out the "Research Plan" worksheet (WS 6.4).
- Ask learners to highlight or circle "Pre-Assessment" at the top of the page.
- Assess understanding with the "Engage Think Competencies Rubric" (Appendix A.6).

THINK LESSON

Objective

Learners will find information that shows different perspectives of foxes.

AASL Standards Framework for Learners: VI.A.3. Learners follow ethical and legal guidelines for gathering and using information by evaluating information for accuracy, validity, social and cultural context, and appropriateness for need.

Lesson Duration

50–60 minutes

Materials

- Library database
- "Foxes" anchor chart (AC 6.5)
- Markers
- Informational books about foxes
- "Fox KWL Chart" worksheet (WS 6.5)
- Pencils
- "Engage Think Competencies Rubric" (Appendix A.6)

Foxes

How I Feel	What I Learned
» Foxes are tricky.	» Foxes want to take care of their babies.
» You can't trust a fox.	» Foxes need shelter and food just like other animals.
» Foxes are always looking for something to eat.	» Foxes are not always a nuisance.

Lesson

1. Engage learners by asking them how they feel about foxes. Write responses on the "Foxes" anchor chart (AC 6.5). Say, "Today we are going to read a book that invites us to see foxes differently. This story has no words. The illustrations do all the talking. Let's take a look at what the pictures are saying."

2. Ask the following questions as you read the book. Record responses on the "Foxes" anchor chart (AC 6.5).
   - "How does the author want us to feel about the fox? How do you know?" (cover)
   - "Has your opinion changed about the fox?" (pp. 1–2)
   - "What is happening on these pages? What would you do if a fox was at your door?" (pp. 5–6)
   - "What do you notice on these pages?" (pp. 7–8)
   - "What do you predict is in the basket?" (pp. 9–10)
   - "What's happening on these pages?" (pp. 13–14)
   - "What do you predict will happen next?" (pp. 17–18)
   - "How do you feel about foxes now? What was the author's purpose for writing this book?" (pp. 23–24)

3. Say, "When we do research, it's important to read different books about the topic because some authors may change the way we think about something. They may give us information that we never thought of before. For example, *Fox's Garden* made me realize that foxes are not always sinister. They have families and need to take care of them just like other animals do."

4. Explain that today learners are going to visit the library database and read books about foxes to learn more about them.

5. Distribute the "Fox KWL Chart" worksheet (WS 6.5). Tell learners to fill out the first two columns before doing research. They will write what they already know about foxes in the "What I Know" portion of the table and what they wonder about foxes in the "What I Wonder" column. New information will be recorded in the "What I Learned" column to show what students learned.

6. Assess questions with the "Engage Think Competencies Rubric" (Appendix A.6).

CREATE LESSON

Objective
Learners will cite where they found their information.

AASL Standards Framework for Learners: VI.B.2. Learners use valid information and reasoned conclusions to make ethical decisions in the creation of knowledge by acknowledging authorship and demonstrating respect for the intellectual property of others.

Lesson Duration
45–50 minutes

Materials

- "Citing Sources" anchor chart (AC 6.6)
- Markers
- "What I Learned, Where I Learned It" worksheet (WS 6.6)
- Pencils
- Access to library books
- *Wonderopolis,* an **AASL Best Website for Teaching and Learning**
- "Engage Create Competencies Rubric" (Appendix A.6)

 Citing Sources

Books

Last Name, First Name. Book Title. Year published.

» Tuttle, Merlin. *The Secret Life of Bats.* 2016.

Websites with No Authors

"Title of the Article." Name of Website. Copyright date. Web.

» "Do Bats Need Maps?" Wonderopolis. 2014–2018. Web.

 Citations are shortened to support young learners.

Lesson

1. Ask learners to think of a piece of art they made that makes them proud. Ask them to imagine someone taking their art and claiming he made it. Ask, "How would you feel?" Explain that authors feel the same way when people take ideas from their books or websites and don't give them credit.
2. Explain that the learners' job is to do some research on a topic of their choice. They can read books or visit *Wonderopolis.*
3. Model reading an interesting fact from a book. Demonstrate how to make note of the fact and cite the source. Write the example on the "Citing Sources" anchor chart (AC 6.6). Follow the same steps while reading *Do Bats Need Maps?* on *Wonderopolis.*
4. Pass out the "What I Learned, Where I Learned It" worksheet (WS 6.6). Read the directions with learners and answer any questions.
5. Assess responses with the "Engage Create Competencies Rubric" (Appendix A.6).

SHARE LESSON

Objective
Learners will debate whether foxes should be feared with a "Sticky Note Tug of War."

AASL Standards Framework for Learners: VI.C.2. Learners responsibly, ethically, and legally share new information with a global community by disseminating new knowledge through means appropriate for the intended audience.

Lesson Duration
45–50 minutes

Materials
- "Should We Be Afraid of Foxes?" anchor chart (AC 6.7)
- Sticky notes
- Pencils
- "Fox KWL Chart" worksheet from the first lesson (WS 6.5)
- "Engage Share Competencies Rubric" (Appendix A.6)

ANCHOR CHART 6.7

Should We Be Afraid of Foxes?

I Am Afraid of Foxes	I Am Not Afraid of Foxes

Lesson

1. Distribute the "Fox KWL Chart" worksheet (WS 6.5) from the first lesson in the unit along with sticky notes and pencils.
2. Instruct learners to put their initials on one sticky note.
3. Ask learners if they think we should be afraid of foxes. If their answer is "yes," they should place their sticky note in the "I Am Afraid of Foxes" column of the "Should We Be Afraid of Foxes?" anchor chart (AC 6.7). If their answer is "no," they should put their sticky note in the "I Am Not Afraid of Foxes" column of the "Should We Be Afraid of Foxes?" anchor chart (AC 6.7).
4. Tell learners that they are going to play a game of "Sticky Note Tug of War." Learners will take turns explaining their vote. They will try to persuade others to feel the same way they do about foxes. If learners are persuaded by the speaker's argument, they will move their sticky note to the other column. For example, if my sticky note is in the "Yes" column but I hear a great reason that persuades me to change my mind, I would move my sticky note to the "No" column.
5. Assess conversations with the "Engage Share Competencies Rubric" (Appendix A.6).

GROW LESSON

Objective

Learners will inform others to read widely for information by using an online tool to present a quotation.

AASL Standards Framework for Learners: VI.D.3. Learners engage with information to extend personal learning by inspiring others to engage in safe, responsible, ethical, and legal information behaviors.

Lesson Duration

45–50 minutes

Materials

- "Research Advice" anchor chart (AC 6.8)
- Markers
- *QuotesCover*
- Computer lab or mobile devices
- Projector
- "Engage Grow Competencies Rubric" (Appendix A.6)

Research Advice

» Read different resources.   » Find material you can understand.

» Cite the information.   » Ask for help.

» Ask questions.

Lesson

1. Introduce the lesson by telling learners that another class is coming to the library to do animal research. Say, "Since you just finished researching an animal, what advice do you have for the other class? What should learners know about researching?" Write responses on the "Research Advice" anchor chart (AC 6.8).

2. Inform learners that you found a quotation that works with research: "When I do research, I cast my net very widely and then snatch what feels right out of that." State that the quotation is from an author named Brandon Sanderson. Ask what they think the quotation means.

3. Explain that you would like learners to decorate the quotation and make it visually appealing. Say, "Because we are using someone's quotation, we need to add that person's name. Why is that important?"

4. Demonstrate how to access *QuotesCover*. Model how to write a quotation and add the author's name.

5. Assess proficiency with the "Engage Grow Competencies Rubric" (Appendix A.6).

Post-Assessment

- Pass out the "Research Plan" worksheet (WS 6.4).
- Ask learners to circle the word "Post-Assessment" at the top of the page to distinguish this from the initial assessment.
- Assess understanding with the "Engage Think Competencies Rubric" (Appendix A.6).
- Compare results with the pre-assessment.

WORKSHEET 6.4

RESEARCH PLAN

Name: _____

Pre-Assessment/Post-Assessment

What is the best plan of action to take when researching a topic you feel strongly about?

_____

_____

_____

_____

_____

_____

_____

_____

_____

_____

_____

_____

_____

WORKSHEET 6.5

FOX KWL CHART

Name: _____

Fox KWL Chart

What I Know about Foxes	What I Wonder about Foxes	What I Learned about Foxes

Did your thinking change as you read more material?   **YES**   **NO**

WHAT I LEARNED, WHERE I LEARNED IT

Name: _____

Directions: What would you like to learn about today? Write the topic on the line below. Read books or visit *Wonderopolis* (https://wonderopolis.org/) to find new information. Write what you learned in the table below. Add where you found the information by citing the author, the title, the website, and a publishing date. Refer to the citation examples in the table.

Research Topic: _____

What I Learned	Where I Learned It
	Book Example: Tuttle, Merlin. *The Secret Life of Bats*. 2016. **Website Example:** "Do Bats Need Maps?" *Wonderopolis*. 2014–2018. Web.
• _____	• _____
• _____	• _____
• _____	• _____
• _____	• _____
• _____	• _____

WHO OWNS AN IDEA?

Shared Foundation: Engage
Featured Book: *In the Bag! Margaret Knight Wraps It Up*
by Monica Kulling

Summary

Machines are pretty cool, especially when they make a job easier, like folding paper into paper bags. Margaret Knight was consumed with inventing machines and tools to make life easier and safer. She made her first invention in 1850. During this time, Knight's work was not respected because she was a woman, and women were not seen as equal in the workforce. Her boss did not give her credit for her inventions, and one idea was stolen. Learn how Margaret Knight fought to claim her invention in this interesting book. Readers will enjoy the illustrations that are reminiscent of an old cartoon movie. They'll appreciate the lesson about protecting ideas and giving credit when it's deserved. After reading this book that touches on intellectual property, children will practice finding copyright-friendly images for school projects.

Pre-Assessment

- Pass out the "Citing Images" worksheet (WS 6.7).
- Ask learners to highlight or circle "Pre-Assessment" at the top of the page.
- Instruct learners to fill out the "What I Wonder about Citing Images" column.
- Assess responses with the "Engage Create Competencies Rubric" (Appendix A.6).

THINK LESSON

Objective

Learners will search for an image about inventions.

AASL Standards Framework for Learners: VI.A.2. Learners follow ethical and legal guidelines for gathering and using information by understanding the ethical use of information, technology, and media.

Lesson Duration

45–50 minutes

Materials

- Copy of *In the Bag! Margaret Knight Wraps It Up* by Monica Kulling
- "What Does an Inventor Do?" anchor chart (AC 6.9)
- Pencils
- "Margaret Knight" worksheet (WS 6.8)
- "Engage Think Competencies Rubric" (Appendix A.6)

ANCHOR CHART 6.9

 What Does an Inventor Do?

» Reads	» Looks for solutions to problems
» Studies	» Draws illustrations
» Works on a project for a long time	» Plans

Lesson

1. Introduce the lesson by asking learners if they have invented something. Explain that you are going to read a story about someone who loved to work on inventions. As you read *In the Bag! Margaret Knight Wraps It Up,* ask learners to notice what an inventor does. Write their responses on the "What Does an Inventor Do?" anchor chart (AC 6.9).
2. Ask the following questions as you read the story:
   - "Look at the illustration. What does it tell us about when this story takes place?" (p. 2)
   - "What questions do you have?" (p. 4)
   - "What do you notice about Mattie?" (p. 6)
   - "What did you learn about Mattie so far?" (p. 8)
   - "What are you thinking about what the neighbors said about Mattie?" (p. 10)
   - "What are we learning about inventors so far?" (p. 12)
   - "How would you describe Mattie?" (p. 18)
   - "What are we learning about inventions?" (pp. 19–24)
3. Ask, "If Margaret Knight walked into this room, what advice do you think she could give us about inventing? What questions would you have for her?" Learners will write their responses on the "Margaret Knight" worksheet (WS 6.8).
4. Assess responses with the "Engage Think Competencies Rubric" (Appendix A.6).

CREATE LESSON

Objective
Learners will cite images.

AASL Standards Framework for Learners: VI.B.2. Learners use valid information and reasoned conclusions to make ethical decisions in the creation of knowledge by acknowledging authorship and demonstrating respect for the intellectual property of others.

Lesson Duration
45–50 minutes

Materials
- Computer lab or mobile devices
- *Pixabay,* an **AASL Best Website for Teaching and Learning**
- *Photos for Class,* an **AASL Best Website for Teaching and Learning**
- "My Image Citations" worksheet (WS 6.9)
- "Format to Cite an Image" anchor chart (AC 6.10)
- Markers
- Pencils
- "Engage Create Competencies Rubric" (Appendix A.6)

ANCHOR CHART 6.10

 Format to Cite an Image

Creator's last name, Creator's first name. "Title of image." *Name of website,* URL.

EXAMPLE: Wellington, Jill. "Brown Eggs, Milk, Breakfast." Pixabay, https://pixabay.com/en/brown-eggs-milk-breakfast-nutrition-3217675/.

No Title?

Describe the image.

EXAMPLE: 12019. Photograph of sheep in Ireland. Pixabay, https://pixabay.com/en/ireland-sheep-lambs-livestock-1985088/.

To make citing images easier for young learners, require only a few elements of a citation. Asking for the author's name and the title of the website where the image was found is a great way to scaffold this skill.

Lesson

1. Engage learners by asking them why someone would think it was acceptable to steal Margaret Knight's paper bag maker idea.
2. Explain that some people take ideas and say it was theirs to begin with. Others take images and use them online without mentioning who took the pictures. Explain that this is wrong. Tell learners that they should always mention the photographer's name. They should also check to make sure that they can borrow the image in the first place. Explain that they are going to visit two sites that allow students to borrow their images.
3. Show learners how to access *Pixabay*. Describe the site as a safe place for learners to find and use images for projects. They have permission to use all the photos on the site. Explain that some images don't require attribution, meaning that learners don't have to mention the author's name. It would be nice to give the photographer credit if the name is available. Demonstrate how to find the author's name by clicking on the top right corner of the page. Explain that some photographers use a number or a username.
4. Point out that it's important to mention the website where learners found the image.
5. Show learners how to access *Photos for Class*. Describe the site as another safe place to find and use images for projects. Point out that when learners download an image, the citation is automatically added. There is also a link to view the photograph on *Pixabay*.
6. Choose an image from one of the sites and demonstrate how to cite the information. Model how to find the author's name. Explain that if the author's name is not listed, learners might find a username instead. If no title is listed, learners should describe the image. Record examples on the "Format to Cite an Image" anchor chart (AC 6.10).
7. Explain that learners will now practice searching for images and citing them. Distribute the "My Image Citations" worksheet (WS 6.9).
8. Assess proficiency with the "Engage Create Competencies Rubric" (Appendix A.6).

SHARE LESSON

Objective

Learners will create a how-to demonstration about citing images.

AASL Standards Framework for Learners: VI.C.1. Learners responsibly, ethically, and legally share new information with a global community by sharing information resources in accordance with modification, reuse, and remix policies.

Lesson Duration
50–60 minutes

Materials
- Computer lab
- Projector
- Mobile devices
- *Seesaw* app, an **AASL Best App for Teaching and Learning**
- *Pixabay,* an **AASL Best Website for Teaching and Learning**
- *Photos for Class,* an **AASL Best Website for Teaching and Learning**
- "Informing Others about Using Images" anchor chart (AC 6.11)
- "Engage Share Competencies Rubric" (Appendix A.6)

ANCHOR CHART 6.11

 Informing Others about Using Images

What should be in our demonstrations to show others how to find and cite images for projects?

» An explanation of why it's important to give photographers credit for their work

» Safe sites to find images for projects

» A demonstration of where to find the author's name and the title of an image

» Examples of citations

⭐ Set up the **Seesaw** app ahead of time with the collaborating educator. **Seesaw** creates QR codes for each class. Print copies of the QR codes for easy access.

Lesson
1. Introduce the lesson by explaining that many people don't realize they must mention where an image came from when they borrow it. Ask learners if they would like to inform others about citing images. Invite learners to share what they would include in their informative presentations. Write responses on the "Informing Others about Using Images" anchor chart (AC 6.11).

2. Tell learners that they will use the *Seesaw* app to demonstrate how to cite information.
3. Ask, "What information should we include in our *Seesaw* presentations?"
4. Instruct learners to use the *Pixabay* and *Photos for Class* websites to find an image for their presentations.
5. Demonstrate how to take a screenshot of an image.
6. Model how to open the *Seesaw* app and find learners' account. Demonstrate how to upload the image to the app. Show learners the different tools that *Seesaw* offers and explain how to cite the image.
7. Assess presentations with the "Engage Share Competencies Rubric" (Appendix A.6).

GROW LESSON

Objective
Learners will find a photo to go with a favorite poem and write a citation.

AASL Standards Framework for Learners: VI.D.2. Learners engage with information to extend personal learning by reflecting on the process of ethical generation of knowledge.

Lesson Duration
3 lessons, 50–60 minutes each

Materials
- "Citing Poetry and Images" anchor chart (AC 6.12)
- Markers
- Poetry books
- "Poetry Citations" worksheet (WS 6.10)
- *Seesaw* app, an **AASL Best App for Teaching and Learning**
- Mobile devices
- *Pixabay,* an **AASL Best Website for Teaching and Learning**
- *Photos for Class,* an **AASL Best Website for Teaching and Learning**
- "Engage Grow Competencies Rubric" (Appendix A.6)

Citing Poetry and Images

Citing Poetry

Poet's last name, Poet's first name. "Title of Poem." Title of Book, page number.

EXAMPLE: Florian, Douglas. "Bees Buzz." unBEElievables, p. 22.

Citing Images

Creator's last name, Creator's first name. "Title of image." Name of website, URL.

EXAMPLE: Wellington, Jill. "Brown Eggs, Milk, Breakfast." Pixabay, https://pixabay.com/en/brown-eggs-milk-breakfast-nutrition-3217675/.

No Title?

Describe the image.

EXAMPLE: 12019. Photograph of sheep in Ireland. Pixabay, https://pixabay .com/en/ireland-sheep-lambs-livestock-1985088/.

Lesson Day 1

1. Engage learners by reading a fun poem. Ask them to pay attention to their mental image as you read the poem. What did they see?
2. Explain that today they will find a favorite poem and write a citation.
3. Model how to write a citation using the poem you read to the class. Record steps on the "Citing Poetry and Images" anchor chart (AC 6.12).
4. Pass out the "Poetry Citations" worksheet (WS 6.10).

Lesson Day 2

1. Read another poem. Ask learners to share the mental images they saw as you read the poem.
2. Tell learners that today they will choose an image to go with their poem. They will use *Pixabay* or *Photos for Class* to find their images. They will upload the picture on the *Seesaw* app and type a citation on the image. Model the steps using the "Citing Poetry and Images" anchor chart as a guide (AC 6.12).

Lesson Day 3

1. Tell learners that today they will add the poem to the picture. They can record their voice reading the poem, or they can type the poem. Instruct learners to add the citations for both the poem and the picture.
2. Assess citations with the "Engage Grow Competencies Rubric" (Appendix A.6).

Post-Assessment

- Pass out the "Citing Images" worksheet (WS 6.7).
- Direct learners to circle the word "Post-Assessment" at the top of the page to distinguish this from the initial assessment.
- Instruct learners to complete the "What I Learned about Citing Images" column.
- Assess responses with the "Engage Create Competencies Rubric" (Appendix A.6).

.

WORKSHEET 6.7

CITING IMAGES

Name: _____

Pre-Assessment/Post-Assessment

Directions:

- **Pre-assessment**—Write what you wonder about citing images in the left-hand column.
- **Post-assessment**—Write what you learned about citing images in the right-hand column.

PRE-ASSESSMENT What I Wonder about Citing Images	POST-ASSESSMENT What I Learned about Citing Images
• _____	• _____
• _____	• _____
• _____	• _____
• _____	• _____
• _____	• _____
• _____	• _____
• _____	• _____
• _____	• _____
• _____	• _____
• _____	• _____
• _____	• _____

MARGARET KNIGHT

Name: _____

Directions: Pretend that you could ask Margaret Knight for advice about the invention process. What advice would she give you? What questions would you ask her? Write your responses on the lines below.

Advice:

- _____

- _____

- _____

- _____

- _____

- _____

- _____

Questions:

- _____

- _____

- _____

- _____

- _____

- _____

- _____

MY IMAGE CITATIONS

Name: _____

Directions:
- Visit the Pixabay (https://pixabay.com) and *Photos for Class* (www.photos forclass.com) websites.
- Find an image about "inventions."

What is the creator's last name? _____

What is the creator's first name? _____

Is there a title of the image? _____

What website did you use to find the image? _____

Put it all together!

This is the format:
- Creator's last name, Creator's first name. "Title of image." Name of website, URL.

Sometimes photographers use numbers or other characters in place of their name. See the example below by photographer "12019."

Examples:
- Wellington, Jill. "Brown Eggs, Milk, Breakfast." Pixabay, https://pixabay.com/en/brown-eggs-milk-breakfast-nutrition-3217675/.
- 12019. Photograph of sheep in Ireland. Pixabay, https://pixabay.com/en/ireland-sheep-lambs-livestock-1985088/.

Now you try!

_____

_____

_____

_____

POETRY CITATIONS

Name: _____

Directions: Find a favorite poem.

What is the author's last name? _____

What is the author's first name? _____

What is the title of the poem? _____

What is the title of the book? _____

What page is the poem on? _____

Put it all together!

This is the format:
- Poet's last name, Poet's first name. "Title of Poem." Title of Book, page number.

This is an example:
- Florian, Douglas. "Bees Buzz." unBEElievables, p. 22.

Now you try!

_____

_____

_____

_____

_____

_____

APPENDIX A
Rubrics

A.1

I. INQUIRE—Build new knowledge by inquiring, thinking critically, identifying problems, and developing strategies for solving problems.

	BEGINNER 1 Point	DEVELOPING 2 Points	ADVANCING 3 Points	COMPETENT 4 Points
A. Think—Learners display curiosity and initiative by:				
1. Formulating questions about a personal interest or a curricular topic. 2. Recalling prior and background knowledge.	With guidance and support, learner attempts to formulate a question.	With minimal support, learner formulates a question related to the topic.	Learner independently formulates a question with a basic connection to background knowledge.	Learner formulates high-quality, relevant questions closely linked to background knowledge.
B. Create—Learners engage with new knowledge by following a process that includes:				
1. Using evidence to investigate questions. 2. Devising and implementing a plan to fill knowledge gaps. 3. Generating products that illustrate learning.	With guidance and support, learner develops a learning plan, supported by evidence to answer questions.	With minimal support, learner develops a learning plan, supported by evidence to answer questions.	Learner independently develops a learning plan, finds evidence for investigation, and creates an illustrative product.	Learner develops a learning plan, finds evidence, and creates a connected, high-quality illustrative product.
C. Share—Learners adapt, communicate, and exchange learning products with others in a cycle that includes:				
1. Interacting with content presented by others. 2. Providing constructive feedback. 3. Acting on feedback to improve. 4. Sharing products with an authentic audience.	With guidance and support, learner interacts and shares content with an authentic audience and accepts feedback.	With minimal guidance and support, learner interacts and shares content with an authentic audience and gives and accepts constructive feedback.	Learner independently interacts and shares content with an authentic audience and gives and acts on constructive feedback.	Learner independently interacts and shares high-quality content with an authentic audience and gives and acts on constructive feedback.
D. Grow—Learners participate in an ongoing inquiry-based process by:				
1. Continually seeking knowledge. 2. Engaging in sustained inquiry. 3. Enacting new understanding through real-world connections. 4. Using reflection to guide informed decisions.	With guidance and support, learner seeks new learning connected to the real world.	With minimal guidance and support, learner seeks knowledge through sustained inquiry and connects with the real world.	Learner independently seeks knowledge through sustained inquiry and connects with the real world. Reflection informs inquiry decisions.	Learner independently initiates high-quality inquiry through real-world connections. Multiple reflections are used to guide learning.

Total Score: Competent: 13–16; Advancing: 9–12; Developing: 5–8; Beginner: 1–4

247

I. INQUIRE—Build new knowledge by inquiring, thinking critically, identifying problems, and developing strategies for solving problems.

	BEGINNER 1 Point	**DEVELOPING** 2 Points	**ADVANCING** 3 Points	**COMPETENT** 4 Points
A. Think—Learners display curiosity and initiative by:				
1. Formulating questions about a personal interest or a curricular topic. 2. Recalling prior and background knowledge.	With guidance and support, learner attempts to formulate a question.	With minimal support, learner formulates a question related to the topic.	Learner independently formulates a question with a basic connection to background knowledge.	Learner formulates high-quality, relevant questions closely linked to background knowledge.

Student: _____ Score: _____

I. INQUIRE—Build new knowledge by inquiring, thinking critically, identifying problems, and developing strategies for solving problems.

	BEGINNER 1 Point	**DEVELOPING** 2 Points	**ADVANCING** 3 Points	**COMPETENT** 4 Points
B. Create—Learners engage with new knowledge by following a process that includes:				
1. Using evidence to investigate questions. 2. Devising and implementing a plan to fill knowledge gaps. 3. Generating products that illustrate learning.	With guidance and support, learner develops a learning plan, supported by evidence to answer questions.	With minimal support, learner develops a learning plan, supported by evidence to answer questions.	Learner independently develops a learning plan, finds evidence for investigation, and creates an illustrative product.	Learner develops a learning plan, finds evidence, and creates a connected, high-quality illustrative product.

Student: _____ Score: _____

I. INQUIRE—Build new knowledge by inquiring, thinking critically, identifying problems, and developing strategies for solving problems.

	BEGINNER 1 Point	DEVELOPING 2 Points	ADVANCING 3 Points	COMPETENT 4 Points
C. Share—Learners adapt, communicate, and exchange learning products with others in a cycle that includes:				
1. Interacting with content presented by others. 2. Providing constructive feedback. 3. Acting on feedback to improve. 4. Sharing products with an authentic audience.	With guidance and support, learner interacts and shares content with an authentic audience and accepts feedback.	With minimal guidance and support, learner interacts and shares content with an authentic audience and gives and accepts constructive feedback.	Learner independently interacts and shares content with an authentic audience and gives and acts on constructive feedback.	Learner independently interacts and shares high-quality content with an authentic audience and gives and acts on constructive feedback.

Student: _____ Score: _____

- -

I. INQUIRE—Build new knowledge by inquiring, thinking critically, identifying problems, and developing strategies for solving problems.

	BEGINNER 1 Point	DEVELOPING 2 Points	ADVANCING 3 Points	COMPETENT 4 Points
D. Grow—Learners participate in an ongoing inquiry-based process by:				
1. Continually seeking knowledge. 2. Engaging in sustained inquiry. 3. Enacting new understanding through real-world connections. 4. Using reflection to guide informed decisions.	With guidance and support, learner seeks new learning connected to the real world.	With minimal guidance and support, learner seeks knowledge through sustained inquiry and connects with the real world.	Learner independently seeks knowledge through sustained inquiry and connects with the real world. Reflection informs inquiry decisions.	Learner independently initiates high-quality inquiry through real-world connections. Multiple reflections are used to guide learning.

Student: _____ Score: _____

II. INCLUDE—Demonstrate an understanding of and commitment to inclusiveness and respect for diversity in the learning community.

	BEGINNER 1 Point	DEVELOPING 2 Points	ADVANCING 3 Points	COMPETENT 4 Points
A. Think—Learners contribute a balanced perspective when participating in a learning community by:				
1. Articulating an awareness of the contributions of a range of learners. 2. Adopting a discerning stance toward points of view and opinions expressed in information resources and learning products. 3. Describing their understanding of cultural relevancy and placement within the global learning community.	With guidance and support, learner attempts to formulate an opinion or stance.	With minimal support, learner formulates an opinion or stance based on new learning.	Learner independently formulates an opinion or stance with a basic connection to cultural relevance.	Learner formulates high-quality opinion based on evidence from new learning, and includes a global focus.
B. Create—Learners adjust their awareness of the global learning community by:				
1. Interacting with learners who reflect a range of perspectives. 2. Evaluating a variety of perspectives during learning activities. 3. Representing diverse perspectives during learning activities.	With guidance and support, learner engages in learning activities while being respectful of varying perspectives.	With minimal support, learner participates in learning activities and shares perspectives from her stance in the global community.	Learner independently participates in learning activities and shares and evaluates various perspectives during learning activities.	Learner shares and evaluates various perspectives during learning activities, and synthesizes various perspectives into own stance.
C. Share—Learners exhibit empathy with and tolerance for diverse ideas by:				
1. Engaging in informed conversation and active debate. 2. Contributing to discussions in which multiple viewpoints on a topic are expressed.	With guidance and support, learner participates in debate and conversation through listening and limited conversation.	With minimal guidance and support, learner discusses one viewpoint and participates in limited conversation.	Learner independently engages in conversations with multiple viewpoints.	Learner independently and respectfully engages in conversations with multiple viewpoints, asking clarifying questions.
D. Grow—Learners demonstrate empathy and equity in knowledge building within the global learning community by:				
1. Seeking interactions with a range of learners. 2. Demonstrating interest in other perspectives during learning activities. 3. Reflecting on their own place within the global learning community.	With guidance and support, learner respectfully listens to multiple perspectives on a topic.	With minimal guidance and support, learner engages in conversation and learning activities with others.	Learner independently seeks out opportunities to work with a range of learners and demonstrates interest in others' perspectives during learning activities.	Learner independently seeks out opportunities to work with a range of learners and demonstrates interest in others' perspectives during learning activities. Learner has awareness of his or her place within the global learning community.

Total Score: Competent 13–16; Advancing 9–12; Developing 5–8; Beginner 1–4

II. INCLUDE—Demonstrate an understanding of and commitment to inclusiveness and respect for diversity in the learning community.

	BEGINNER 1 Point	**DEVELOPING** 2 Points	**ADVANCING** 3 Points	**COMPETENT** 4 Points
A. Think—Learners contribute a balanced perspective when participating in a learning community by:				
1. Articulating an awareness of the contributions of a range of learners. 2. Adopting a discerning stance toward points of view and opinions expressed in information resources and learning products. 3. Describing their understanding of cultural relevancy and placement within the global learning community.	With guidance and support, learner attempts to formulate an opinion or stance.	With minimal support, learner formulates an opinion or stance based on new learning.	Learner independently formulates an opinion or stance with a basic connection to cultural relevance.	Learner formulates high-quality opinion based on evidence from new learning, and includes a global focus.

Student: _____ Score: _____

II. INCLUDE—Demonstrate an understanding of and commitment to inclusiveness and respect for diversity in the learning community.

	BEGINNER 1 Point	**DEVELOPING** 2 Points	**ADVANCING** 3 Points	**COMPETENT** 4 Points
B. Create—Learners adjust their awareness of the global learning community by:				
1. Interacting with learners who reflect a range of perspectives. 2. Evaluating a variety of perspectives during learning activities. 3. Representing diverse perspectives during learning activities.	With guidance and support, learner engages in learning activities while being respectful of varying perspectives.	With minimal support, learner participates in learning activities and shares perspectives from her or his stance in the global community.	Learner independently participates in learning activities and shares and evaluates various perspectives during learning activities.	Learner shares and evaluates various perspectives during learning activities, and synthesizes various perspectives into own stance.

Student: _____ Score: _____

II. INCLUDE—Demonstrate an understanding of and commitment to inclusiveness and respect for diversity in the learning community.

	BEGINNER 1 Point	**DEVELOPING** 2 Points	**ADVANCING** 3 Points	**COMPETENT** 4 Points
C. Share—Learners exhibit empathy with and tolerance for diverse ideas by:				
1. Engaging in informed conversation and active debate. **2. Contributing to discussions in which multiple viewpoints on a topic are expressed.**	With guidance and support, learner participates in debate and conversation through listening and limited conversation.	With minimal guidance and support, learner discusses one viewpoint and participates in limited conversation.	Learner independently engages in conversations with multiple viewpoints.	Learner independently and respectfully engages in conversations with multiple viewpoints, asking clarifying questions.

Student: _____ Score: _____

- -

II. INCLUDE—Demonstrate an understanding of and commitment to inclusiveness and respect for diversity in the learning community.

	BEGINNER 1 Point	**DEVELOPING** 2 Points	**ADVANCING** 3 Points	**COMPETENT** 4 Points
D. Grow—Learners demonstrate empathy and equity in knowledge building within the global learning community by:				
1. Seeking interactions with a range of learners. **2. Demonstrating interest in other perspectives during learning activities.** **3. Reflecting on their own place within the global learning community.**	With guidance and support, learner respectfully listens to multiple perspectives on a topic.	With minimal guidance and support, learner engages in conversation and learning activities with others.	Learner independently seeks out opportunities to work with a range of learners and demonstrates interest in others' perspectives during learning activities.	Learner independently seeks out opportunities to work with a range of learners and demonstrates interest in others' perspectives during learning activities. Learner has awareness of his or her place within the global learning community.

Student: _____ Score: _____

III. COLLABORATE—Work effectively with others to broaden perspectives and work toward common goals.

	BEGINNER 1 Point	DEVELOPING 2 Points	ADVANCING 3 Points	COMPETENT 4 Points
A. Think—Learners identify collaborative opportunities by:				
1. Demonstrating their desire to broaden and deepen understandings. 2. Developing new understandings through engagement in a learning group. 3. Deciding to solve problems informed by group interaction.	With guidance and support, learner develops new understandings by being part of a group.	With minimal support, learner deepens understanding and participates in a group to learn more.	Learner independently demonstrates initiative to deepen understandings through engaged work in learning groups.	Learner independently demonstrates initiative to deepen understandings and solves problems informed through engaged work in learning groups.
B. Create—Learners participate in personal, social, and intellectual networks by:				
1. Using a variety of communication tools and resources. 2. Establishing connections with other learners to build on their own prior knowledge and create new knowledge.	With guidance and support, learner connects prior knowledge to new learning.	With minimal support, learner connects prior knowledge to new learning and connects with other learners.	Learner independently connects prior knowledge with new learning, works with other learners, and uses at least two varieties of communication tools and resources.	Learner independently connects prior knowledge with new learning, works with other learners, and uses more than two varieties of communication tools and resources.
C. Share—Learners work productively with others to solve problems by:				
1. Soliciting and responding to feedback from others. 2. Involving diverse perspectives in their own inquiry processes.	With guidance and support, learner engages in the inquiry process and accepts feedback.	With minimal guidance and support, learner engages in the inquiry process, involving diverse perspectives. Learner accepts feedback.	Learner independently engages in the inquiry process, involving diverse perspectives. Learner solicits and responds to feedback.	Learner independently engages in the inquiry process, involving diverse perspectives. Learner solicits high-quality feedback and response is specific.
D. Grow—Learners actively participate with others in learning situations by:				
1. Actively contributing to group discussions. 2. Recognizing learning as a social responsibility.	With guidance and support, learner listens and responds sporadically to group discussions.	With minimal guidance and support, learner listens and responds with short answers.	Learner independently contributes to group discussions, offering high-quality ideas with evidence to support.	Learner independently initiates high-quality discussions, provides evidence, and recognizes learning as a social responsibility.

Total Score: Competent 13–16; Advancing 9–12; Developing 5–8; Beginner 1–4

III. COLLABORATE—Work effectively with others to broaden perspectives and work toward common goals.

	BEGINNER 1 Point	DEVELOPING 2 Points	ADVANCING 3 Points	COMPETENT 4 Points
A. Think—Learners identify collaborative opportunities by:				
1. Demonstrating their desire to broaden and deepen understandings. 2. Developing new understandings through engagement in a learning group. 3. Deciding to solve problems informed by group interaction.	With guidance and support, learner develops new understandings by being part of a group.	With minimal support, learner deepens understanding and participates in a group to learn more.	Learner independently demonstrates initiative to deepen understandings through engaged work in learning groups.	Learner independently demonstrates initiative to deepen understandings and solves problems informed through engaged work in learning groups.

Student: _____ Score: _____

- -

III. COLLABORATE—Work effectively with others to broaden perspectives and work toward common goals.

	BEGINNER 1 Point	DEVELOPING 2 Points	ADVANCING 3 Points	COMPETENT 4 Points
B. Create—Learners participate in personal, social, and intellectual networks by:				
1. Using a variety of communication tools and resources. 2. Establishing connections with other learners to build on their own prior knowledge and create new knowledge.	With guidance and support, learner connects prior knowledge to new learning.	With minimal support, learner connects prior knowledge to new learning and connects with other learners.	Learner independently connects prior knowledge with new learning, works with other learners, and uses at least two varieties of communication tools and resources.	Learner independently connects prior knowledge with new learning, works with other learners, and uses more than two varieties of communication tools and resources.

Student: _____ Score: _____

III. COLLABORATE—Work effectively with others to broaden perspectives and work toward common goals.

	BEGINNER 1 Point	**DEVELOPING** 2 Points	**ADVANCING** 3 Points	**COMPETENT** 4 Points
C. Share—Learners work productively with others to solve problems by:				
1. Soliciting and responding to feedback from others. 2. Involving diverse perspectives in their own inquiry processes.	With guidance and support, learner engages in the inquiry process and accepts feedback.	With minimal guidance and support, learner engages in the inquiry process, involving diverse perspectives. Learner accepts feedback.	Learner independently engages in the inquiry process, involving diverse perspectives. Learner solicits and responds to feedback.	Learner independently engages in the inquiry process, involving diverse perspectives. Learner solicits high-quality feedback and response is specific.

Student: _____ Score: _____

III. COLLABORATE—Work effectively with others to broaden perspectives and work toward common goals.

	BEGINNER 1 Point	**DEVELOPING** 2 Points	**ADVANCING** 3 Points	**COMPETENT** 4 Points
D. Grow—Learners actively participate with others in learning situations by:				
1. Actively contributing to group discussions. 2. Recognizing learning as a social responsibility.	With guidance and support, learner listens and responds sporadically to group discussions.	With minimal guidance and support, learner listens and responds with short answers.	Learner independently contributes to group discussions, offering high-quality ideas with evidence to support.	Learner independently initiates high-quality discussions, provides evidence, and recognizes learning as a social responsibility.

Student: _____ Score: _____

A.4

IV. CURATE—Make meaning for oneself and others by collecting, organizing, and sharing resources of personal relevance.

	BEGINNER 1 Point	DEVELOPING 2 Points	ADVANCING 3 Points	COMPETENT 4 Points
A. Think—Learners act on an information need by:				
1. Determining the need to gather information. 2. Identifying possible sources of information. 3. Making critical choices about information sources to use.	With guidance and support, learner identifies various sources of information.	With minimal support, learner identifies sources of information and makes choices about which source to use.	Learner independently determines a variety of information sources and identifies the most pertinent sources of information.	Learner independently identifies a need, determines a variety of information sources across media formats, and identifies the most pertinent sources of information.
B. Create—Learners gather information appropriate to the task by:				
1. Seeking a variety of sources. 2. Collecting information representing diverse perspectives. 3. Systematically questioning and assessing the validity and accuracy of information. 4. Organizing information by priority, topic, or other systematic scheme.	With guidance and support, learner asks questions to determine the validity and accuracy of information.	With minimal support, learner seeks a variety of resources with diverse perspectives. Learner asks questions and assesses the validity and accuracy of information.	Learner seeks a variety of resources with diverse perspectives. Learner asks questions and assesses the validity and accuracy of information and organizes information in a systematic scheme.	Learner independently seeks and collects a variety of resources with diverse perspectives. Learner asks questions and assesses the validity and accuracy of information and organizes information in a systematic scheme.
C. Share—Learners exchange information resources within and beyond their learning community by:				
1. Accessing and evaluating collaboratively constructed information sites. 2. Contributing to collaboratively constructed information sites by ethically using and reproducing others' work. 3. Joining with others to compare and contrast information derived from collaboratively constructed information sites.	With guidance and support, learner interacts with collaboratively constructed information sites.	With minimal guidance and support, learner interacts with and evaluates collaboratively constructed information sites. Learner ethically uses and reproduces others' work.	Learner independently accesses and evaluates collaboratively constructed information sites. Learner ethically uses and reproduces others' work. Learner joins with others to discuss information.	Learner independently accesses and evaluates collaboratively constructed information sites. Learner ethically uses and reproduces others' work. Learner joins with others to compare and contrast information.
D. Grow—Learners select and organize information for a variety of audiences by:				
1. Performing ongoing analysis of and reflection on the quality, usefulness, and accuracy of curated resources. 2. Integrating and depicting in a conceptual knowledge network their understanding gained from resources. 3. Openly communicating curation processes for others to use, interpret, and validate.	With guidance and support, learner reflects on the quality, usefulness, and accuracy of curated resources.	With minimal guidance and support, learner reflects on the quality, usefulness, and accuracy of curated resources. Learner integrates conceptual knowledge from resources.	Learner independently reflects on the quality, usefulness, and accuracy of curated resources. Learner integrates conceptual knowledge from resources.	Learner independently reflects on the quality, usefulness, and accuracy of curated resources. Learner integrates conceptual knowledge from resources. Learner communicates the curation process.

Total Score: Competent 13–16; Advancing 9–12; Developing 5–8; Beginner 1–4

IV. CURATE—Make meaning for oneself and others by collecting, organizing, and sharing resources of personal relevance.

	BEGINNER 1 Point	DEVELOPING 2 Points	ADVANCING 3 Points	COMPETENT 4 Points
A. Think—Learners act on an information need by:				
1. Determining the need to gather information. 2. Identifying possible sources of information. 3. Making critical choices about information sources to use.	With guidance and support, learner identifies various sources of information.	With minimal support, learner identifies sources of information and makes choices about which source to use.	Learner independently determines a variety of information sources and identifies the most pertinent sources of information.	Learner independently identifies a need, determines a variety of information sources across media formats, and identifies the most pertinent sources of information.

Student: _____ Score: _____

- -

IV. CURATE—Make meaning for oneself and others by collecting, organizing, and sharing resources of personal relevance.

	BEGINNER 1 Point	DEVELOPING 2 Points	ADVANCING 3 Points	COMPETENT 4 Points
B. Create—Learners gather information appropriate to the task by:				
1. Seeking a variety of sources. 2. Collecting information representing diverse perspectives. 3. Systematically questioning and assessing the validity and accuracy of information. 4. Organizing information by priority, topic, or other systematic scheme.	With guidance and support, learner asks questions to determine the validity and accuracy of information.	With minimal support, learner seeks a variety of resources with diverse perspectives. Learner asks questions and assesses the validity and accuracy of information.	Learner seeks a variety of resources with diverse perspectives. Learner asks questions and assesses the validity and accuracy of information and organizes information in a systematic scheme.	Learner independently seeks and collects a variety of resources with diverse perspectives. Learner asks questions and assesses the validity and accuracy of information and organizes information in a systematic scheme.

Student: _____ Score: _____

IV. CURATE—Make meaning for oneself and others by collecting, organizing, and sharing resources of personal relevance.

	BEGINNER 1 Point	DEVELOPING 2 Points	ADVANCING 3 Points	COMPETENT 4 Points
C. Share—Learners exchange information resources within and beyond their learning community by:				
1. Accessing and evaluating collaboratively constructed information sites. 2. Contributing to collaboratively constructed information sites by ethically using and reproducing others' work. 3. Joining with others to compare and contrast information derived from collaboratively constructed information sites.	With guidance and support, learner interacts with collaboratively constructed information sites.	With minimal guidance and support, learner interacts with and evaluates collaboratively constructed information sites. Learner ethically uses and reproduces others' work.	Learner independently accesses and evaluates collaboratively constructed information sites. Learner ethically uses and reproduces others' work. Learner joins with others to discuss information.	Learner independently accesses and evaluates collaboratively constructed information sites. Learner ethically uses and reproduces others' work. Learner joins with others to compare and contrast information.

Student: _____ Score: _____

IV. CURATE—Make meaning for oneself and others by collecting, organizing, and sharing resources of personal relevance.

	BEGINNER 1 Point	DEVELOPING 2 Points	ADVANCING 3 Points	COMPETENT 4 Points
D. Grow—Learners select and organize information for a variety of audiences by:				
1. Performing ongoing analysis of and reflection on the quality, usefulness, and accuracy of curated resources. 2. Integrating and depicting in a conceptual knowledge network their understanding gained from resources. 3. Openly communicating curation processes for others to use, interpret, and validate.	With guidance and support, learner reflects on the quality, usefulness, and accuracy of curated resources.	With minimal guidance and support, learner reflects on the quality, usefulness, and accuracy of curated resources. Learner integrates conceptual knowledge from resources.	Learner independently reflects on the quality, usefulness, and accuracy of curated resources. Learner integrates conceptual knowledge from resources.	Learner independently reflects on the quality, usefulness, and accuracy of curated resources. Learner integrates conceptual knowledge from resources. Learner communicates the curation process.

Student: _____ Score: _____

A.5

V. EXPLORE—Discover and innovate in a growth mindset developed through experience and reflection.

	BEGINNER 1 Point	DEVELOPING 2 Points	ADVANCING 3 Points	COMPETENT 4 Points
A. Think—Learners develop and satisfy personal curiosity by:				
1. Reading widely and deeply in multiple formats and write and create for a variety of purposes. 2. Reflecting and questioning assumptions and possible misconceptions. 3. Engaging in inquiry-based processes for personal growth.	With guidance and support, learner engages in inquiry process through reading across sources, and conveys new thinking on an inquiry topic.	With minimal support, learner engages in inquiry process, reads, writes, and/or creates across sources, with limited awareness of misconceptions.	Learner independently engages in inquiry process, reads, writes, and creates across formats while reflecting on assumptions and misconceptions.	Learner engages in high quality inquiry, while reflecting and questioning assumptions. Additionally, student reads, writes, and creates across formats for a variety of purposes.
B. Create—Learners construct new knowledge by:				
1. Problem solving through cycle of design, implementation, and reflection. 2. Persisting through self-directed pursuits by tinkering and making.	With guidance and support, learner develops a problem-solving plan that includes tinkering and making.	With minimal support, learner develops and engages in parts of a problem-solving plan that includes tinkering and making.	Learner independently develops and engages in parts of a problem-solving plan that includes tinkering and making.	Learner independently develops and persists through a problem-solving cycle of design, implementation, and reflection that includes self-directed tinkering and making.
C. Share—Learners engage with the learning community by:				
1. Expressing curiosity about a topic of personal interest or curricular relevance. 2. Co-constructing innovative means of investigation 3. Collaboratively identifying innovative solutions to a challenge or problem.	With guidance and support, learner expresses curiosity about an interest and develops a plan for investigation.	With minimal guidance and support, learner expresses curiosity about an interest, develops a plan for investigation, and begins to identify solutions to a challenge.	Learner independently expresses curiosity about an interest, develops an innovative plan for investigation, and begins to identify solutions to a challenge.	Learner independently expresses curiosity about an interest, develops an innovative plan for investigation, and begins to collaboratively identify innovative solutions to a challenge.
D. Grow—Learners develop through experience and reflection by:				
1. Iteratively responding to challenges. 2. Recognizing capabilities and skills that can be developed, improved, and expanded. 3. Open-mindedly accepting feedback for positive and constructive growth.	With guidance and support, learner accepts feedback and responds to challenges.	With minimal guidance and support, learner accepts feedback and responds to challenges.	Learner independently accepts feedback, responds to challenges, and identifies skills and capabilities for development.	Learner independently seeks out feedback for growth, responds to challenges, and makes a plan for skill and capability development.

Total Score: Competent 13–16; Advancing 9–12; Developing 5–8; Beginner 1–4

V. EXPLORE—Discover and innovate in a growth mindset developed through experience and reflection.

	BEGINNER 1 Point	**DEVELOPING** 2 Points	**ADVANCING** 3 Points	**COMPETENT** 4 Points
A. Think—Learners develop and satisfy personal curiosity by:				
1. Reading widely and deeply in multiple formats and write and create for a variety of purposes. 2. Reflecting and questioning assumptions and possible misconceptions. 3. Engaging in inquiry-based processes for personal growth.	With guidance and support, learner engages in inquiry process through reading across sources, and conveys new thinking on an inquiry topic.	With minimal support, learner engages in inquiry process, reads, writes, and/or creates across sources, with limited awareness of misconceptions.	Learner independently engages in inquiry process, reads, writes, and creates across formats while reflecting on assumptions and misconceptions.	Learner engages in high quality inquiry while reflecting and questioning assumptions. Additionally, student reads, writes, and creates across formats for a variety of purposes.

Student: _____ Score: _____

- -

V. EXPLORE—Discover and innovate in a growth mindset developed through experience and reflection.

	BEGINNER 1 Point	**DEVELOPING** 2 Points	**ADVANCING** 3 Points	**COMPETENT** 4 Points
B. Create—Learners construct new knowledge by:				
1. Problem solving through cycle of design, implementation, and reflection. 2. Persisting through self-directed pursuits by tinkering and making.	With guidance and support, learner develops a problem-solving plan that includes tinkering and making.	With minimal support, learner develops and engages in parts of a problem-solving plan that includes tinkering and making.	Learner independently develops and engages in parts of a problem-solving plan that includes tinkering and making.	Learner independently develops and persists through a problem-solving cycle of design, implementation, and reflection that includes self-directed tinkering and making.

Student: _____ Score: _____

V. EXPLORE—Discover and innovate in a growth mindset developed through experience and reflection.

	BEGINNER 1 Point	**DEVELOPING** 2 Points	**ADVANCING** 3 Points	**COMPETENT** 4 Points
C. Share—Learners engage with the learning community by:				
1. Expressing curiosity about a topic of personal interest or curricular relevance. 2. Co-constructing innovative means of investigation. 3. Collaboratively identifying innovative solutions to a challenge or problem.	With guidance and support, learner expresses curiosity about an interest and develops a plan for investigation.	With minimal guidance and support, learner expresses curiosity about an interest, develops a plan for investigation, and begins to identify solutions to a challenge.	Learner independently expresses curiosity about an interest, develops an innovative plan for investigation, and begins to identify solutions to a challenge.	Learner independently expresses curiosity about an interest, develops an innovative plan for investigation, and begins to collaboratively identify innovative solutions to a challenge.

Student: _____ Score: _____

- -

V. EXPLORE—Discover and innovate in a growth mindset developed through experience and reflection.

	BEGINNER 1 Point	**DEVELOPING** 2 Points	**ADVANCING** 3 Points	**COMPETENT** 4 Points
D. Grow—Learners develop through experience and reflection by:				
1. Iteratively responding to challenges. 2. Recognizing capabilities and skills that can be developed, improved, and expanded. 3. Open-mindedly accepting feedback for positive and constructive growth.	With guidance and support, learner accepts feedback and responds to challenges.	With minimal guidance and support, learner accepts feedback and responds to challenges.	Learner independently accepts feedback, responds to challenges, and identifies skills and capabilities for development.	Learner independently seeks out feedback for growth, responds to challenges, and makes a plan for skill and capability development.

Student: _____ Score: _____

A.6

VI. ENGAGE—Demonstrate safe, legal, and ethical creating and sharing of knowledge products independently while engaging in a community of practice and an interconnected world.

	BEGINNER 1 Point	DEVELOPING 2 Points	ADVANCING 3 Points	COMPETENT 4 Points
A. Think—Learners follow ethical and legal guidelines for gathering and using information by:				
1. Responsibly applying information, technology, and media to learning. 2. Understanding the ethical use of information, technology, and media. 3. Evaluating information for accuracy, validity, social and cultural context, and appropriateness for need.	With guidance and support, learner attempts to find and evaluate resources for accuracy, validity, and the appropriateness for need.	With minimal support, learner responsibly evaluates resources for accuracy, validity, and the appropriateness for need.	Learner independently and responsibly evaluates resources for accuracy, validity, and the appropriateness for need.	Learner independently and responsibly evaluates and applies accurate and appropriate information with understanding of context and appropriateness for need.
B. Create—Learners use valid information and reasoned conclusions to make ethical decisions in the creation of knowledge by:				
1. Ethically using and reproducing others' work. 2. Acknowledging authorship and demonstrating respect for the intellectual property of others. 3. Including elements in personal-knowledge products that allow others to credit content appropriately.	With guidance and support, learner acknowledges the authorship of intellectual property when reproducing others' work.	With minimal support, learner acknowledges the authorship of intellectual property when reproducing others' work and includes credit statements.	Learner independently acknowledges the authorship of intellectual property when reproducing others' work and includes credit statements.	Learner independently and ethically credits authorship of intellectual property when reproducing others' work and includes accurate and complete credit statements.
C. Share—Learners responsibly, ethically, and legally share new information with a global community by:				
1. Sharing information resources in accordance with modification, reuse, and remix policies. 2. Disseminating new knowledge through means appropriate for the intended audience.	With guidance and support, learner interacts and shares content through means appropriate for intended audience.	With minimal guidance and support, learner interacts and shares content with an intended audience with some consideration given to modification, reuse, and remix policies.	Learner independently interacts and shares content through means appropriate for intended audience with most resources in accordance with modification, reuse, and remix policies.	Learner independently interacts and shares content through means appropriate for intended audience fully in accordance with modification, reuse, and remix policies.
D. Grow—Learners engage with information to extend personal learning by:				
1. Personalizing their use of information and information technologies. 2. Reflecting on the process of ethical generation of knowledge. 3. Inspiring others to engage in safe, responsible, ethical, and legal information behaviors.	With guidance and support, learner initiates ethical generation of knowledge.	With minimal guidance and support, learner seeks knowledge through sustained inquiry and connects with the real world.	Learner independently initiates ethical generation of knowledge through personalized information technologies.	Learner independently initiates personalized generation of knowledge while inspiring the safe, ethical, and legal information behaviors in others.

Total Score: Competent 13–16; Advancing 9–12; Developing 5–8; Beginner 1–4

VI. ENGAGE—Demonstrate safe, legal, and ethical creating and sharing of knowledge products independently while engaging in a community of practice and an interconnected world.

	BEGINNER 1 Point	DEVELOPING 2 Points	ADVANCING 3 Points	COMPETENT 4 Points
A. Think—Learners follow ethical and legal guidelines for gathering and using information by:				
1. Responsibly applying information, technology, and media to learning. 2. Understanding the ethical use of information, technology, and media. 3. Evaluating information for accuracy, validity, social and cultural context, and appropriateness for need.	With guidance and support, learner attempts to find and evaluate resources for accuracy, validity, and the appropriateness for need.	With minimal support, learner responsibly evaluates resources for accuracy, validity, and the appropriateness for need.	Learner independently and responsibly evaluates resources for accuracy, validity, and the appropriateness for need.	Learner independently and responsibly evaluates and applies accurate and appropriate information with understanding of context and appropriateness for need.

Student: _____ Score: _____

- -

VI. ENGAGE—Demonstrate safe, legal, and ethical creating and sharing of knowledge products independently while engaging in a community of practice and an interconnected world.

	BEGINNER 1 Point	DEVELOPING 2 Points	ADVANCING 3 Points	COMPETENT 4 Points
B. Create—Learners use valid information and reasoned conclusions to make ethical decisions in the creation of knowledge by:				
1. Ethically using and reproducing others' work. 2. Acknowledging authorship and demonstrating respect for the intellectual property of others. 3. Including elements in personal-knowledge products that allow others to credit content appropriately.	With guidance and support, learner acknowledges the authorship of intellectual property when reproducing others' work.	With minimal support, learner acknowledges the authorship of intellectual property when reproducing others' work and includes credit statements.	Learner independently acknowledges the authorship of intellectual property when reproducing others' work and includes credit statements.	Learner independently and ethically credits authorship of intellectual property when reproducing others' work and includes accurate and complete credit statements.

Student: _____ Score: _____

VI. ENGAGE—Demonstrate safe, legal, and ethical creating and sharing of knowledge products independently while engaging in a community of practice and an interconnected world.

	BEGINNER 1 Point	DEVELOPING 2 Points	ADVANCING 3 Points	COMPETENT 4 Points
C. Share—Learners responsibly, ethically, and legally share new information with a global community by:				
1. Sharing information resources in accordance with modification, reuse, and remix policies. 2. Disseminating new knowledge through means appropriate for the intended audience.	With guidance and support, learner interacts and shares content through means appropriate for intended audience.	With minimal guidance and support, learner interacts and shares content with an intended audience with some consideration given to modification, reuse, and remix policies.	Learner independently interacts and shares content through means appropriate for intended audience with most resources in accordance with modification, reuse, and remix policies.	Learner independently interacts and shares content through means appropriate for intended audience fully in accordance with modification, reuse, and remix policies.

Student: _____ Score: _____

- -

VI. ENGAGE—Demonstrate safe, legal, and ethical creating and sharing of knowledge products independently while engaging in a community of practice and an interconnected world.

	BEGINNER 1 Point	DEVELOPING 2 Points	ADVANCING 3 Points	COMPETENT 4 Points
D. Grow—Learners engage with information to extend personal learning by:				
1. Personalizing their use of information and information technologies. 2. Reflecting on the process of ethical generation of knowledge. 3. Inspiring others to engage in safe, responsible, ethical, and legal information behaviors.	With guidance and support, learner initiates ethical generation of knowledge.	With minimal guidance and support, learner seeks knowledge through sustained inquiry and connects with the real world.	Learner independently initiates ethical generation of knowledge through personalized information technologies.	Learner independently initiates personalized generation of knowledge while inspiring the safe, ethical, and legal information behaviors in others.

Student: _____ Score: _____

B.1

PLANNING SHEET

Name: _____

> Ideas I Have
>
>
>
>
>
>
>
> Things I Need
> • _____   • _____
>
> • _____   • _____
>
> • _____   • _____

Steps to Take

1) _____

2) _____

3) _____

4) _____

Self-Assessment

How did you do? Circle the sentence that tells your experience.

| I needed help making a plan. | I had a few questions. | I wrote the plan on my own. |

B.2

REFLECT AND GROW

Name: _____

I am proud of . . .

I had trouble with . . .

I will improve by . . .

B.3

WHAT I NOTICE, WHAT I WONDER

Name: _____

Directions: Write or illustrate your observations in the frame below. Write your
"What I Wonder" questions on the lines provided.

Topic:

What I Notice:

_____

_____

_____

_____

What I Wonder:

_____

_____

_____

_____

HAIKU POEM

Name: _____

Topic: _____

Haiku poetry originated in Japan and is mostly about nature. A haiku poem is made up of three lines. Each line follows a specific pattern of syllables. The first line has five syllables, the second line has seven syllables, and the third line has five syllables.

Here is an example of a haiku poem about sea turtles:

Hatched beneath the sand (5 syllables)
Racing to the shore when born (7 syllables)
The sea is my home (5 syllables)

_____

_____

_____

_____

_____

_____

_____

_____

B.5

THEME POEM

Name:

Topic:

What is the topic of your poem? Can you draw an outline of the topic? If so, you have the beginning of a theme poem. Write a poem about the topic along the outline or inside the outline.

B.6

ACROSTIC POEM

Name: _____

Topic: _____

Poetry gives us the freedom to share our knowledge in a creative way. An acrostic poem has a simple template to get you started. Begin by writing the topic in a vertical direction from top to bottom. After each letter, write something that describes the topic, starting with that letter.

Here's an example of an acrostic poem about flags:

Flying high
Lasting symbol
Always remember
Grand

_____

_____

_____

_____

_____

_____

_____

_____

_____

_____

B.7

VENN DIAGRAM

Name: _____

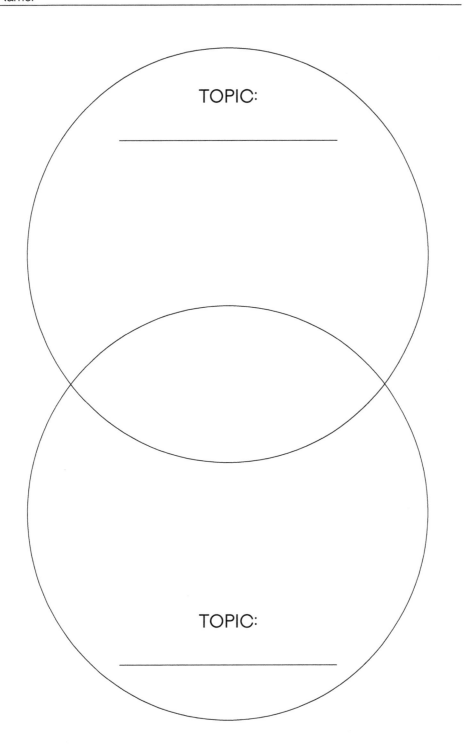

TOPIC:

_____

TOPIC:

_____

B.8

SELF-DESIGNED RESEARCH ACTIVITY

What do you want to learn about?

How do you plan to learn it?

How do you plan to share your learning?

B.9

OPINION

Name: _____

Did you change your opinion, or did it stay the same after the class discussion?

_____

If you changed your opinion, answer these questions:

I used to think . . .

_____

_____

But now I think . . .

_____

_____

I changed my mind because . . .

_____

_____

If you did not change your opinion, complete the following:

I did not change my mind because . . .

_____

_____

I heard these ideas that supported my thinking:

1) _____

2) _____

3) _____

B.10

FEEDBACK FOR PROJECTS

Name: _____

Title of Project: _____

Name(s) of Presenter(s): _____

List what you like about the project:

- _____

- _____

- _____

- _____

- _____

Is the message clear? If not, what questions do you have about the project?

_____

_____

_____

_____

What suggestions do you have for improvements?

_____

_____

_____

_____

BIBLIOGRAPHY

American Association of School Librarians. *National School Library Standards for Learners, School Librarians, and School Libraries.* Chicago: ALA Editions, 2018.

Baccelliere, Anna. *I Like, I Don't Like.* Grand Rapids, MI: Eerdmans Books for Young Readers, 2017.

Camcam, Princesse. *Fox's Garden.* New York: Enchanted Lion Books, 2014.

Cannon, Janell. *Stellaluna.* San Diego: Harcourt, 1993.

Cousteau, Philippe. *Follow the Moon Home: A Tale of One Idea, Twenty Kids, and a Hundred Sea Turtles.* San Francisco: Chronicle Books, 2016.

Eggers, Dave. *Her Right Foot.* San Francisco: Chronicle Books, 2017.

Haughton, Chris. *Shh! We Have a Plan.* Somerville, MA: Candlewick Press, 2014.

Hood, Susan. *Ada's Violin: The Story of the Recycled Orchestra of Paraguay.* New York: Simon and Schuster Books for Young Readers, 2016.

Jenson-Elliott, Cindy. *Antsy Ansel: Ansel Adams, a Life in Nature.* New York: Henry Holt, 2016.

Kulling, Monica. *In the Bag! Margaret Knight Wraps It Up.* Toronto: Tundra Books, 2011.

Lacey, Saskia. *How to Build a Plane: A Soaring Adventure of Mechanics, Teamwork, and Friendship.* Lake Forest, CA: Quarto Publishing Group, 2015.

Lamothe, Matt. *This Is How We Do It: One Day in the Lives of Seven Kids from around the World.* San Francisco: Chronicle Books, 2017.

MacKenzie, Emily. *Wanted! Ralfy Rabbit, Book Burglar.* London: Bloomsbury Publishing, 2015.

Markle, Sandra. *Thirsty, Thirsty Elephants.* Watertown, MA: Charlesbridge, 2017.

McCarney, Rosemary. *The Way to School.* Toronto: Second Story Press, 2015.

McDonnell, Patrick. *Me . . . Jane.* New York: Little, Brown, 2011.

Messier, Mireille. *The Branch.* Ontario: Kids Can Press, 2016.

Martin, Jacqueline Briggs. *Farmer Will Allen and the Growing Table.* Bellevue, WA: Readers to Eaters Books, 2013.

Ørbeck-Nilssen, Constance. *Why Am I Here?* Grand Rapids, MI: Eerdmans Books for Young Readers, 2016.

Paul, Miranda. *One Plastic Bag: Isatou Ceesay and the Recycling Women of the Gambia.* Minneapolis: Millbrook Press, 2015.

Peñaranda-Loftus, J. (Producer). *Landfill Harmonic.* Vimeo, 2016.

Sanderson, Brandon. "When I do research, I cast my net very widely and then snatch what feels right out of that." Brandon Sanderson Quotes. BrainyQuote.com, Brainy Media Inc., 2018, https://www.brainyquote.com/quotes/brandon_sanderson _538423.

Savery, Annabel. *My Country Brazil.* London: Franklin Watts, 2013.

Schwartz, Joanne. *Town Is by the Sea.* Toronto; Berkeley, CA: Groundwood Books, 2017.

Siddals, Mary McKenna. *Compost Stew: An A to Z Recipe for the Earth.* Berkeley, CA: Tricycle Press, 2010.

Spires, Ashley. *The Most Magnificent Thing.* Toronto: Kids Can Press, 2014.

Sweet, Melissa. *Balloons Over Broadway: The True Story of the Puppeteer of Macy's Parade.* Boston: Houghton Mifflin Books for Children, 2011.

Wenzel, Brendan. *They All Saw a Cat.* San Francisco: Chronicle Books, 2016.

ONLINE RESOURCES

The following list is in alphabetical order by book title. The online resources that support each lesson follow the title.

How Do People and Groups Decide How to Make the World a Better Place?

Ada's Violin: The Story of the Recycled Orchestra of Paraguay by Susan Hood

Flipgrid (https://info.flipgrid.com/)

Kidblog (https://kidblog.org/home/)

Landfill Harmonic (https://vimeo.com)

Seesaw (https://web.seesaw.me/platforms)

Tellagami (https://tellagami.com/)

How Can We Collect Important Information to Share with Others?

Antsy Ansel: Ansel Adams, a Life in Nature by Cindy Jenson-Elliott

Google Expeditions (https://support.google.com/edu/expeditions/
    answer/6335093?hl=en)

Padlet (https://padlet.com/)

The Hidden Worlds of the National Parks (https://artsandculture.withgoogle.com/en-us/
    national-parks-service/parks)

How Can We Work Together to Repurpose Materials?

The Branch by Mireille Messier

DIY (https://diy.org/)

Seesaw (https://web.seesaw.me/)

How Can We Reduce Waste?

Compost Stew: An A to Z Recipe for the Earth by Mary McKenna Siddals

Garbology (www.naturebridge.org/garbology.php)

Photos for Class (www.photosforclass.com)

Why Is It Important to Find Innovative Solutions to Problems?

Farmer Will Allen and the Growing Table by Jacqueline Briggs Martin

Ross, Matthew. "Vermicomposting: How Worms Can Reduce Our Waste." TED-Ed. June
2013. Animation. (https://ed.ted.com/lessons/vermicomposting-how-worms-can
-reduce-our-waste-matthew-ross#watch)

How Can People Identify Problems?

Follow the Moon Home: A Tale of One Idea, Twenty Kids, and a Hundred Sea Turtles
by Philippe Cousteau

Padlet (https://padlet.com/dashboard)

What Causes People to Have Certain Feelings about Different Animals?

Fox's Garden by Princesse Camcam

QuotesCover (https://quotescover.com/)

Wonderopolis (https://wonderopolis.org/wonder/do-bats-need-maps)

What Makes a Team Successful?

How to Build a Plane: A Soaring Adventure of Mechanics, Teamwork, and Friendship
by Saskia Lacey

Curiosity Machine: Inspiration Video (https://www.curiositymachine.org/challenges/
111/)

Wonderopolis: How Far Can a Paper Airplane Fly? (https://wonderopolis.org/wonder/
how-far-can-a-paper-airplane-fly)

Who Owns an Idea?

In the Bag! Margaret Knight Wraps It Up by Monica Kulling

Photos for Class (www.photosforclass.com)

Pixabay (https://pixabay.com)

Seesaw (https://web.seesaw.me/platforms)

How Can We Record Our Observations?

Me . . . Jane by Patrick McDonnell

"Citizen Scientists: Resources to Find the Perfect Project," a *Knowledge Quest* blog post
(http://knowledgequest.aasl.org/citizen-scientists-resources-find-perfect-project/)

GarageBand (https://www.apple.com/ios/garageband/)

Jane Goodall's Roots and Shoots (https://www.rootsandshoots.org/aboutus)

MusicQuest (https://www.musiquest.com/)

Poets.org (https://www.poets.org/poetsorg/collection/poetic-forms)
Tellagami (https://itunes.apple.com/us/app/tellagami/id572737805?mt=8)
Youth Service America (https://ysa.org/)

How Can People Find Solutions to Problems in Their Community?

One Plastic Bag: Isatou Ceesay and the Recycling Women of the Gambia by Miranda Paul
DIY (https://diy.org/)
Wonderopolis (https://wonderopolis.org/)

How Can Listening to Ideas Help Us Develop a Successful Plan?

Shh! We Have a Plan by Chris Haughton
Creatubbles (https://www.creatubbles.com/users/zBKu9Qi5/creations)

How Does Our Background Influence Perception?

They All Saw a Cat by Brendan Wenzel
Bookopolis (https://www.bookopolis.com/#/)
Photos for Class (www.photosforclass.com/)
Pixabay (https://pixabay.com/)
Seesaw app (https://web.seesaw.me/platforms/)

Why Is It Important to Use Multiple Sources to Learn about a Topic?

Thirsty, Thirsty Elephants by Sandra Markle
O'Connell-Rodwell, Caitlin. "The Family Structure of Elephants." TED-Ed. November
    2013. Lecture. (https://ed.ted.com/lessons/the-family-structure-of-elephants
    -caitlin-o-connell-rodwell#discussion)
Padlet (https://padlet.com/)
Wonderopolis (https://wonderopolis.org/)

What Influences People to Live and Work in Our Community?

Town Is by the Sea by Joanne Schwartz
Google Maps (https://www.google.com/maps)
Piktochart (https://piktochart.com/)

Why Is It Important to Keep Track of What We Read and What We Want to Read?

Wanted! Ralfy Rabbit, Book Burglar by Emily MacKenzie
Bookopolis (https://www.bookopolis.com)

What Can We Learn about a Society by Understanding How Students Get to School?

The Way to School by Rosemary McCarney

DK Find Out! (https://www.dkfindout.com/us/)

On the Way to School, Amazon Prime Video (https://www.amazon.com/Way-School
-Jackson-Saikong/dp/B077XKZ4JR/ref=sr_1_1?s=instant-video&ie=UTF8&qid
=1529716385&sr=1-1&keywords=On+the+way+to+school)

How Do People Decide Where to Live?

Why Am I Here? by Constance Ørbeck-Nilssen

Google Maps Street View Treks, an AASL Best Website for Teaching and Learning (https://
www.google.com/maps/about/treks/#/grid)

INDEX

CPSIA information can be obtained
at www.ICGtesting.com
Printed in the USA
FFHW020911090120
57559561-62957FF

9 780838 917756